Men-at-Arms • 546

The Red Army 1922–41

From Civil War to 'Barbarossa'

Philip Jowett • Illustrated by Stephen Walsh

Series editors Martin Windrow & Nick Reynolds

OSPREY PUBLISHING
Bloomsbury Publishing Plc
Kemp House, Chawley Park, Cumnor Hill, Oxford OX2 9PH, UK
29 Earlsfort Terrace, Dublin 2, Ireland
1385 Broadway, 5th Floor, New York, NY 10018, USA
E-mail: info@ospreypublishing.com
www.ospreypublishing.com

OSPREY is a trademark of Osprey Publishing Ltd

First published in Great Britain in 2022

A catalogue record for this book is available from the British Library

ISBN: PB: 9781472850454; eBook: 9781472850447;
ePDF: 9781472850430; XML: 9781472850461

22 23 24 25 26   10 9 8 7 6 5 4 3 2 1
Editor: Martin Windrow
Index by Alan Rutter
Typeset by PDQ Digital Media Solutions, Bungay, UK
Printed in India by Replika Press Private Ltd.

Osprey Publishing supports the Woodland Trust, the UK's leading woodland
conservation charity.

To find out more about our authors and books, visit
www.ospreypublishing.com. Here you will find extracts, author interviews,
details of forthcoming events, and the option to sign up for our newsletter.

Dedication

This book is respectfully dedicated to my dearly loved Uncle John, 1938–2021.

Acknowledgements

I would like to acknowledge my debt to the following researchers into Russian
military history: Chris Nelson, Nikolai Roginsky, Ilya Savchenkov, Anton Shalito,
Kiryl Tsyplenkov, and David Webster. My thanks go, as always, to Paul V. Walsh,
for his help with this and a number of my previous Osprey titles.
All the photographs are from my personal collection, and all are in the
public domain.

Artist's note

Readers may care to note that the original paintings from which the colour
plates in this book were prepared are available for private sale. All reproduction
copyright whatsoever is retained by the publisher. All enquiries should be
addressed to:
http://www.stephenwalshillustrations.co.uk
The publishers regret that they can enter into no correspondence upon
this matter.

TITLE PAGE
Crew of a Maxim M1910 machine gun photographed in 1938, wearing the
M1936 steel helmet. With its wide-flaring frontal brim, this appears to have been
inspired by the Swiss Army's M1918, though with the addition of a very small
'comb' on the apex. The collar patches are in Rifles raspberry-red piped with
black, and bear no insignia for privates. These soldiers have full equipment,
including the German-style M1930 knapsack with the blanket roll strapped
around its top and sides. From 1939 this pack would be replaced with a lighter
canvas M1938, and most knapsacks seem to have been discarded from field
dress early in World War II. (Author's collection) .

OPPOSITE
**An officer ('commander') and his deputy pose for a studio
photograph in 1922, as the Civil War comes to an end. They
wear service caps of different shades, with metal red star
badges. On the left forearm of his standing-collar field shirt
the seated officer displays a single red cloth square centred
below a red star, identifying him as a *komvzvoda* – platoon
commander. On his left breast is the badge authorized in
July 1918 for all members of the Red Army. with the red star
between silver laurel and oak branches. The other man's
dark garments are difficult to identify; he shows no rank
insignia, but seems to wear on his forearm the silver pick-&-
shovel symbol of the engineer branch. (Author's collection)**

THE RED ARMY 1922-41

From Civil War to 'Barbarossa'

INTRODUCTION

The Russian 'Red Army of Workers and Peasants' (RKKA) that emerged victorious from five years of civil war in late 1922 was a huge but poorly armed and equipped force. It was described at the time by the Western press as an 'armed rabble', and (despite the obvious bias) with some justification. However, the fact remained that this patchily trained and equipped army had won a bitter civil war against counter-revolutionary 'White' forces which at one time totalled some half a million men. Although their dispersion and disunity of command eventually proved fatal to them, the Whites had been more professionally officered, and, for most of the Civil War, much better armed than the RKKA.

The Red Army had also defeated (or simply outlasted) a number of interventionist foreign forces sent to help the White armies defeat the Revolution in northern and southern Russia, totalling some 120,000 men. Additionally, a Czech Legion of up to 60,000 men, created in Tsarist Russia from former Austro–Hungarian prisoners of war and Imperial Russian Army veterans, had also fought its way against the Bolsheviks right across Siberia; and Japan had also committed about 70,000 troops to eastern Siberia right up until 1922.

By the time of the close of major operations late in that year, the RKKA was at the very least 3.5 million strong. While predominantly infantry, it also included strong cavalry and artillery branches, a small mechanized force, plus a few other technical units and a small air arm. After an initial massive reduction, over the next 19 years the Red Army was to develop into one of the largest and most powerful in the world. Although it did not fight a major conflict during the 1920s or early 1930s, its troops were embroiled in a number of campaigns during a period that saw the imposition of Bolshevik rule over the whole of the former Russian Empire, and in the late 1930s the Red Army would again face foreign enemies.

THE RED ARMY IN THE 1920s

Strength

As Commissar for Military and Naval Affairs from March 1918, Leon Trotsky had been the architect of the Red Army during the Civil War which lasted until November 1922.[1] However, after the Bolshevik leader Lenin fell seriously ill in March 1923 Trotsky's position was weakened, and, during the power struggle that followed until and after Lenin's death in January 1924, he effectively lost control over the RKKA. His demand for a 1.5 million-strong army in 1921–22 had proved unaffordable due to the desperate state of the economy; in 1922 army strength was fixed at 600,000 men, and by 1923 had fallen to 562,000. Side-lined during 1924 by the new Chairman of the Communist Party, Joseph Stalin, Trotsky was replaced in his post by Mikhail Frunze in January 1925.

Frunze was well aware of the problems facing the army, and stated that its training was not even at the level of the much-maligned Tsarist army pre-1918. Ten per cent of its senior officers had little or no formal education, having joined the Red Army since 1917 as amateur 'street fighters'. During the Civil War their lack of education was partly offset by enrolling about 150,000 former Tsarist professionals as 'military specialists' *(voyenspetzi)* under the close supervision of Party commissars (see p.5), but it was now seen as a major obstacle to the Red Army's modernization. In 1925, about 50 per cent of the senior and technical officers were still former Tsarists; their true loyalty to the Soviet Union was widely doubted, although their lack of connection with their men was supposed to be bridged by the political commissars appointed to serve alongside them.

In 1924, the Red Army was organized in 77 infantry (*strelkovy*, 'rifle') divisions; 31 of these were made up of full-time regulars and the other 46 of part-time 'territorials'. In practice, more than 52 per cent of the RKKA were now a part-time militia force which received little training (again, due to financial constraints).

Clandestine contacts with Germany

Even while the Red Army was battling to crush its last enemies in Central Asia in the early 1920s, following the Treaty of Rapallo in 1922 links began to be forged between the militaries of the Soviet Union and the German Weimar Republic. After 1918 both Russia and Germany were treated by the victorious Entente (Allied) powers as dangerous pariahs. Under the terms of the 1919 Treaty of Versailles, the German Army was limited to 100,000 men without armoured or air support, while that of the Soviet Union – which still furiously resented the pro-White interventions in the Civil War – was seen as a potential threat to the West.

From 1922, in an effort to rebuild their armed forces, the two states secretly shared facilities and aided each other in various ways. The Germans, intent on building a clandestine air force, needed a training base for 50 new Fokker DXIII fighters which they acquired from the Netherlands. In 1926 these were shipped to a new fighter school

---

1   The Gregorian (Western) calendar was adopted by Russia only in February 1918. All dates were advanced by 13 days on 1 February under the 'Old Style' Julian calendar, which was declared to be 14 February under the 'New Style' Gregorian system. Backdating, the storming of the Winter Palace in St Petersburg which began the Bolshevik coup (the 'October Revolution') took place on 25 October 1917 (Old Style), but 7 November 1917 (New Style).

Beginning in 1919, the annual military parade in Moscow was a highlight in the calendar for the Bolshevik regime, which ensured that every effort was made to impress foreign observers. Here smartly turned-out infantrymen march past the reviewing stand in Red Square in 1923. They have winter-weight khaki *budenovka* caps, apparently stiffened at the point, and bearing the crimson cloth star of the Rifles. Their April 1919-pattern khaki *kaftan* greatcoats display matching collar patches and *razgovory* chest tabs. At this stage of the Red Army's development, units as well-dressed as this would be very much the exception to the norm. (Author's collection)

established at Lipetsk in Russia and financed by Germany, and in return Red Army Air Force ground crews were trained by German instructors; Germany also opened the Kama armoured school at Kazan. The secretive nature of this co-operation kept it to a relatively small scale, but it was to continue until Adolf Hitler came to power in 1933.

The role of political commissars

Coinciding with the induction of former Imperial Army officers and senior NCOs into the Red Army from summer 1918, Trotsky established an Institute of Political Commissars. This would provide politically reliable Communist Party members to shadow the line officers of RKKA units at every level of command down to companies. During the early 1920s the Red Army still contained many ex-Tsarist 'specialists', and it was felt essential to keep them under close supervision.

The task of political officers – commissars – was to keep a constant eye on the unit officers' behaviour and attitudes, especially their political reliability. In 1926 the commissar's role was described as being to 'assist the unit commander to maintain discipline; to educate the unit both generally and politically, even when this education borders on military training; and to accept complaints from the personnel.' Effectively, the commissars were political spies, whose adverse reports could lead, at the very least, to a reprimand and a bad mark in an officer's dossier, so it is unsurprising that their relationships with line officers were often strained. A unit commander could not make a decision without consulting his commissar, who often had little or no military education. Commissars also kept a close watch on the rankers of their units, and relied upon loyal Party members among the soldiers to keep them informed.

The effect of this system on officers' morale was noted by the Red Army high command. From 1925, where unit officers were judged to be politically reliable, the role of the commissars was reduced, and some were even removed from units whose commanders were deemed to be particularly loyal. However, commissars were still seen by many officers as an encumbrance to their effective running of their units. During the

Russo–Finnish War of 1939–40 the constant interference of political officers in combat decisions would be one of the factors in the Red Army's poor performance. The negative influence of commissars led to a temporary reduction of their powers from August 1940, but these were strengthened again from June 1941 in an effort to shore up the crumbling RKKA during the German invasion – Operation 'Barbarossa'.

CAMPAIGNS IN THE 1920s
Anti-Basmachi campaigns, 1920s–30s

The Tsarist conquests in Central Asia in the mid to late 19th century had seen vast regions populated by ethnic Turkic peoples added to the Russian Empire. During the Revolution and the Civil War both the Red and White armies had operated in this chaotic theatre of war, where a miscellany of local armed bands rejected the rule of either Reds or Whites. The Red Army's eventual advances (which could not amount to true occupation, given the distances and the required manpower) were seen by most of the Turkic peoples as a threat to their Islamic faith from the atheist government in Moscow. The last passages of the Civil War therefore blurred into post-war rebellions as anti-Bolshevik guerrilla bands sprung up in several Central Asian regions, launching repeated attacks against Red Army garrisons and non-Muslim immigrants.

By 1920 these so-called 'Basmachi' bands had already grown to a strength of at least 20,000 men, and at their peak may have had up to 30,000 guerrillas in the field. However, these formed hundreds of separate bands, from which half-a-dozen major leaders strove to form temporary groupings, and keeping these fed, armed and supplied was a constant challenge for the disunited and rivalrous Basmachi leadership. They were supported for a few years by a government of Afghanistan, but this ended after 1929, when the monarchy of that country was seized by the Russian-allied victor in a civil war. While guerrilla activity was widespread, one major centre lay in the remote Fergana Valley; here some 200 identifiable bands occupied an area of about 8,500 square miles, which has comprised parts of eastern Uzbekistan, southern Kyrgyzstan and northern Tajikistan since the formation of those three Soviet Socialist Republics during 1924–28.

The Bolsheviks sent substantial numbers of troops to Central Asia during the Civil War, and between 1920 and 1923 the total Red Army strength in that theatre, including local auxiliaries, reached between 120,000 and 160,000 men. At times Muslim volunteers formed up to 15 per cent of the anti-Basmachi forces, but many of them changed sides during the campaigns. Foreign volunteers also came to Central Asia to fight for the Basmachi, including Enver Pasha, the former joint leader of the Ottoman regime in 1914–18. Initially serving the Emir of Bukhara, this renowned

The smartly uniformed colour party and lancers of a cavalry unit on parade outside the walls of the Moscow Kremlin in 1922, wearing service caps and the summer version of the standing-collar 1919 *gymnastiorka* field shirt. Three complete Cavalry Armies had played a major part in the Bolsheviks' victory in the Civil War, and throughout the 1920s this branch would remain the principal manoeuvre arm. Before World War I the lance had been general issue throughout the Imperial regular cavalry and Cossacks. (Author's collection)

Photographed in 1923, this Red
Army crew (judging by their
sabres, cavalrymen) are manning
a US Colt-Browning M1895
'potato-digger' machine gun;
each regiment had a mounted
MG squadron. They present an
ethnic mix, with a European gun
commander in the foreground
while the other soldiers are of
Central Asian origin. They also
wear a striking variety of uniform
colours typical of the logistically
chaotic aftermath of the Civil
War. Most of them wear soft
service caps, while the gunner
has a tall early pattern of the
budenovka with a very deep
rear button-up flap. At least two
of the others display the three
coloured *razgovory* chest tabs
ordered in April 1919, and the
man at far right has the collar
patches ordered in January 1922.
(Author's collection)

This snapshot shows a Red Army
unit fighting on the Turkestan
front in 1922. By this date the
main operations of the Civil
War had ended, but there was
still resistance to the Soviet
government in several outlying
regions. Again, the variety of
uniforms underlines the confused
nature of procurement in the
Red Army of this period. Most
of the men wear peaked service
caps, and several have summer
gymnastiorka field shirts in white
cotton or linen. (Author's collection)

military figure assembled a number of Basmachi groups under his command, but he was killed in action in August 1922.

As the Basmachi threat grew during the early 1920s, high-ranking Red Army officers were sent to Central Asia, including the RKKA's *Komandarm* Sergei Kamenev, the Civil War victor over the armies of Adm Kolchak and Gen Denikin. The commitment included a large contingent of the Army Air Force and also a few armoured vehicles, and the former, in particular, began to wear down the rebels' morale. In 1923 several large tribal groups gave up the fight, leaving just a few thousand warriors in the field. By 1925 Tajikistan had been conquered, and 200,000 refugees had fled into Afghanistan.

Just when the Basmachi movement was about to fade out in 1929, the Bolsheviks introduced their policy of forced collectivization of land

ownership, which re-ignited the Basmachi revolts and led to several more years of low-level guerrilla warfare. However, by 1933 even the bulk of the Turkic population saw the few remaining irreconcilables more as simple bandits than as freedom-fighters, and these were suppressed in the spring of that year. During these rebellions the Red Army and its auxiliaries had suffered just under 10,000 deaths, and untold numbers of Muslim fighters and civilians had been killed.

The Sino-Soviet War, 1929

During the same period the Red Army fought another little-known clash in the Soviet Far East. As constituted during the 1920s, the new Soviet Union had immensely long frontiers to defend, with limited forces. In the Far East it faced not only the Imperial Japanese Army, which had a presence in Manchuria, but also a Manchurian-Chinese warlord. Marshal Chang Hsueh-liang was a recent adherent of the Chinese Nationalist government of Chiang Kai-shek, which left him in control of the three provinces of Manchuria.

In 1929 Chang Hsueh-liang decided to challenge Soviet control of the Chinese Eastern Railway, which ran through Manchuria but was owned by the Russians. Skirmishing broke out in July, and on 6 August the RKKA announced formation of the Special Red Banner Far Eastern Army commanded by Vassily Blyukher. To meet the Chinese threat a Trans–Baikal Group was detached from this command, with a strength of 6,000 infantry and 1,600 cavalry; equipment included 166 light and 331 heavy machine guns and 88 field guns, along with a company of nine MS-1 light tanks (also designated T-18 – the first Soviet-designed tank). There was also an air element with 32 aircraft, mostly ex-British DH-9 light bombers. During the conflict the Soviet forces in the whole theatre were expanded to 113,000 men, about 20 per cent of total RKKA strength. They were faced by up to 200,000 poorly armed and trained Manchurian troops, backed by a few thousand White Russian emigré volunteers.

This press picture is reported to be from the 1929 'Sino–Soviet War' between the Soviet Union and the northern Manchurian warlord Chang Hsueh-liang. The troops' uniforms show hard wear and a variety of shades; the greatcoat ordered in 1919 was khaki, and that of the 1922 regulations, grey. The *budenovka* caps seem to be woollen, but cut like the summer type, with front peak and rear flap made in one continuous piece. Their officer (left), wearing a service cap, appears to be the only one displaying crimson infantry-branch collar patches. (Author's collection)

On 17 August, Soviet troops took heavy losses while attempting to storm Manchurian entrenchments at Chalainor under machine-gun fire. During October, Soviet naval advances along the Amur and Songhua rivers forced Manchurian-Chinese forces to fall back. During 17–26 November ten Soviet divisions were deployed successfully against first Chalainor and then Manzhouli, and on 13 December the Chinese government signed a peace agreement. This Soviet victory was hardly reported outside the region, but some military observers were impressed by the Red Army's performance, albeit against inferior opposition.

The 'secret invasion' of Afghanistan, 1929

Also in 1929, a little-known incursion into Afghanistan was launched by Red Army troops from the Central Asian Military District. Their mission was to support King Amanullah Khan, who, after coming to power in 1919, had instituted a number of domestic policies (such as opening schools for girls) which most of the Afghan population deemed far too progressive. Resistance to them contributed to the outbreak of widespread tribal rebellions, and the king appealed to the Soviets for military aid and weapons.

Red Army intelligence officers were not impressed by the standard of the king's troops, and decided that a covert operation in support of the monarch might be a better option. This undercover operation was carried out during April and May by Russian troops dressed like Afghans, with orders not to speak their mother tongue in front of the locals, and led by Red Army officers who assumed Afghan names. This 2,000-strong force was made up largely of cavalry, and was led by the former Civil War Red Cossack commander Vitaly Primakov. Their equipment initially included 24 machine guns and 4 mountain guns, and they were later reinforced by a further 400 men with 6 guns and 8 machine guns. They would also have the support of a few light bombers (presumably with their insignia removed).

Much to their displeasure, the Russians were put under the overall command of an Afghan general, Nabi Khan. They were told that they would be greeted as liberators, but since the civil war was many-sided and chaotic they were instead regarded by the population simply as invaders, and the Afghan rebels received support from among the Basmachi guerrillas who were already fighting the Red Army in Central Asia. Primakov's force succeeded in taking a few towns and defeating several tribal forces sent against it. Fighting continued from mid-April until late May, and the Russian troops were back across the frontier into the Soviet Union by the 28th of that month. On 17 June rebels took Kabul, and the defeated Amanullah Khan went into exile. In October the throne was seized by Muhammed Nadir Khan, who reached an accommodation with the Soviet Union which lasted until his assassination in 1933.

Another rare photograph, showing soldiers of the Trans–Baikal Group detached from the Red Banner Far Eastern Army for the 1929 campaign. The hardest fighting took place in November–December, and several of these men are wearing non-standard sheepskin coats and/or felt *valenki* overboots. Most wear the *budenovka,* but in the uncropped print some fleece hats can also be seen. (Author's collection)

THE RED ARMY IN THE 1930s

Expansion and re-equipment

In 1930 the strength of the Red Army's active regular units in full-time service stood at 562,000, with an additional 842,000 in the part-time territorial reserve. Technical, armoured, artillery and Air Force personnel all served full-time due to the amount of training they required. Hitler's succession to power in Germany in 1933 prompted an immediate decision to raise the active strength considerably. This would be achieved by the forced conversion of two-thirds of the territorial reservists into regular soldiers, and by drafting in conscripts on two-year terms by lowering the age threshold from 21 to 19 years old. During 1934 the number of troops in active units was increased from 885,000 men to 940,000. The order of battle then stood at 82 rifle divisions, 20 cavalry divisions, and a single mechanized division. Of the infantry, 75 per cent were still made up of converted territorials rather than fully trained regulars, although this fact was officially denied. In 1936 total strength rose to 1,300,000 men, and subsequently to 1,600,000.

From June 1934 the People's Commissar for Defence (the defence minister on the Council of People's Commissars, *Sovnarkom*, headed by Stalin) was the cavalry general Kliment Voroshilov. Voroshilov was an ardent follower of Stalin, and was one of the few military commanders whom the 'Man of Steel' trusted. (Nevertheless, he would spend most of his long military career trying to avoid the fate of those of his fellow senior officers who did not enjoy that precarious protection.)

By a law passed in 1936, all the many races that made up the Soviet Union would henceforth be liable for Red Army service including, for the first time, the millions of Muslim citizens. It was planned that 71 of the then-existing 103 rifle divisions should be all-regular formations by January 1938, and that the rest of the territorials would be converted into regulars over the following two years. Soviet sources reported that the standing army had been expanded to 1.5 million men by 1938. On 1 September 1939 the initial age of conscription was dropped to 17 years, the term increased from two to three years, and many previous exemptions for education and family responsibilities were discontinued.

At the turn of the 1920s–30s, soldiers receive instruction in the use of what appears to be a mobile field telephone switchboard. All wear soft-topped 1920s khaki service caps, with mainly summer field shirts and winter trousers. They carry their blankets in a 'horseshoe' roll, but no other equipment. Their collar patches may be black, perhaps with the royal-blue piping of signals troops, but the pinned-on insignia (left foreground) are unidentifiable here. (Author's collection)

Equipping such an expanded and modernizing army obviously presented major challenges. Starting in the late 1920s, Stalin launched a number of industrial initiatives announced as 'three-year' or 'five-year plans'. During the 1st Five-Year Plan (1928–32) the production of military equipment and weaponry was rapidly expanded. In 1930 the total number of military aircraft produced was 860, but two years later it had risen to 2,500. During the same period the production of small arms and new artillery pieces had doubled. The 2nd Five-Year Plan (1933–37) achieved still further expansion of war industries. However, the lack of adequate infrastructure to support this concentration of effort caused problems, and fear of Stalin's tyrannical rule meant that failures to meet targets due to such practical difficulties went unreported. A 3rd Five-Year plan from 1938 was cut short by the outbreak of war with Germany in June 1941.

Cossacks in the Red Army, 1936–41

'Cossack' is not an actual ethnicity, but is best described as a self-identifying historical 'caste'. Under the Russian Empire it had been a long-standing policy to employ the renowned Cossack light cavalry, drawn from communities in the Northern Caucasus, as border troops. As one of the main bulwarks against threats from the south and east, these 'hosts' enjoyed a special relationship with the Romanov dynasty, which repaid their loyalty with privileges and an arm's-length exercise of government authority. Some Cossack communities which settled in the Urals and Siberia performed the same role, but these did not enjoy the same historical heritage as the Don, Kuban and Terek hosts from the Northern Caucasus.

After the fall of the Romanovs in 1917 there was widespread Cossack recruitment into the various White armies in the Civil War, and consequently severe restrictions were imposed by the Bolshevik victors from 1922. Cossacks were not allowed openly to serve in the Red Army, and there were no distinct Cossack units. In April 1936, on Marshal Voroshilov's orders, it was decided to re-name two existing cavalry divisions as 'Cossack divisions' with Don, Kuban and Terek regiments, and further divisions were soon established, reaching 13 in all by the outbreak of war. Any would-be soldier living in the Cossack homelands could now volunteer to serve in these divisions regardless of his actual family origins.

Formation of armoured units, 1922–41

The Red Army had used a handful of captured French and British tanks during the Civil War, but thereafter most emphasis was placed on armoured cars and armoured trains, which were easier to produce in automobile, tractor and train factories. When the time came for the formation of standing mechanized units foreign expertise was

1935: two Red Army cavalrymen show off their Cossack-style *shashka* sabres, without crossguards; these were worn in the 'oriental' manner, slung from a cross-strap and with the cutting edge to the rear. Officially the M1927 *budenovka* was mid-grey, the *gymnastiorka* khaki, and these troopers seem to wear dark blue trousers. The cap badge-backing and collar patches are cavalry-blue, the latter piped in black. (Author's collection)

The raising of ethnic–minority units in the Red Army went in and out of favour at various dates during the interwar years, depending upon the situation in outlying areas. In the 1920s national infantry or cavalry units were raised in Armenia, Georgia, Dagestan and other regions, but most of these were broken up in 1937 as part of a drive to emphasize the unity of the ethnically diverse USSR. Photographed in 1936, this officer commands a Central Asian cavalry unit, possibly patrolling during a small-scale rebellion in Dagestan. His troopers are wearing their traditional turban and striped *kaftan* regularized into a uniform (compare with C2), and the commander also sports a turban with his Red Army field dress. (Author's collection)

essential, and the Red Army looked to a fellow 'rogue' state, Germany, for assistance. In 1928 a German armoured school was set up at Kazan in the Urals, where secretly-built German vehicles were tested, and doctrine was shared. Although a development of the Renault FT-17 tank (the T-18) appeared in 1928, Russia still had virtually no domestic production facilities. Consequently, during 1929–32 Stalin – passionately insistent on industrial modernization – spent huge sums on importing US and German metal-working machinery and setting up factories, and sent engineers abroad for training. Small numbers of European and US tank designs were purchased, and licence-production rights were secured. Developed on these foreign models, prototypes of several light and medium tanks were soon designed, and manufacture began. Despite false starts, by the mid-1930s mass production was under way of T-27 tankettes, T-26 series 'light infantry' tanks, and BT-5 'fast tanks' – and both heavy and improved medium tanks were on the horizon.

There was some opposition at senior levels of the RKKA to the move to develop a mechanized force, since conservative cavalry officers were still convinced of the value of mounted troops. In 1934, Voroshilov told the 17th Party Congress that it was necessary 'once and for all to put an end to the theory of replacing the horse with the machine'. Even five years later, in March 1939, he declared that mounted troops were still important, and that they still 'serve as an example of discipline and military skill' to the rest of the Red Army.

Regardless of these regressive views, the number of tanks produced by Soviet industry was enormously expanded during the 1930s and, under pressure from Voroshilov's talented deputy, the tank enthusiast Gen Mikhail Tukhachevsky, the army plunged into mechanization. During the 1st Five Year Plan the number of tanks produced had risen from 740 to 3,300. By 1935 the Red Army had by far the largest armoured force in the world, with approximately 10,000 tanks and many other AFVs on strength. By that time the RKKA had (at least on paper) 4 mechanized corps, plus 6 independent mechanized brigades, 20 independent tank and mechanized cavalry regiments, 37 tank companies and 27 tankette battalions.

Soviet security forces, 1922–41

Security and intelligence agencies were given the highest priority by the Bolsheviks, whose fear of both external and internal opposition to their newly installed regime amounted to a siege mentality. In 1917 the cadre of the first security police force, the CHEKA – standing for 'All-Russian Extraordinary Commission' – was about 200 strong; by March 1918 it also controlled the Frontier Troops (border guards), and by early 1921 it had expanded to well over 200,000 personnel. In February 1922 the CHEKA was absorbed into a new agency, the GPU – standing for 'State Political Directorate'. Following the expansion of the Russian Soviet Federal Socialist Republic (RSFSR) into the Union of Soviet Socialist Republics (USSR) in December 1922, the GPU became the OGPU – standing for 'Joint State Political Directorate'. It kept this name until 1934, when it became the NKVD – standing for 'People's Commissariat for Internal Affairs'. In 1939 the NKVD was divided into 17 chief directorates, of which State Security (GUGB), and the strong Frontier and Internal Troops (GUPVV) are relevant to this book.[2]

Militarized units of these security agencies had existed since their inception, but the OGPU/NKVD were greatly expanded during the 1920s–30s to fulfill the various roles of a political praetorian guard utterly loyal to Stalin. These included control of the police (GURKM) and the labour-camp system (GULAG), which required not only guards but also many transport/escort units. The growth of the militarized OGPU saw it reach 33 per cent of the strength of the regular Red Army during the early 1930s. OGPU/NKVD units were given priority in equipment and weaponry; by the 1930s many of them were motorized, and by 1941 they could field 14 divisions. Stalin exploited the natural rivalry between the Red Army and the NKVD, playing the leadership of each off against the other.

Stalin's purges, 1934–41

The senior Bolshevik leadership was often riven by conspiratorial rivalries, and the paranoia which surrounded Stalin came to a head in the mid-1930s, following the deaths of millions in the famine caused by the forced collectivization of agricultural land from 1928. The first accusations of treachery made against senior figures came at the turn of 1934–35, and over the following four years a deranged witch-hunt dragged in entire categories of the population accused of being 'enemies of the people'. The flimsiest suspicion of disloyalty at any level brought denunciation as 'class enemies, Trotskyists, spies and saboteurs', and some 200,000 Communist Party members were expelled. Every Russian citizen or resident foreigner, be they a worker, official, intellectual, a member of Stalin's senior circle, or even of the security agency itself, lived in fear of the 'midnight knock on the door'. (During the purges about 20,000 NKVD agents were arrested, and two successive heads of the agency – Genrikh Yagoda and Nikolai Yezhov – were among those executed.)

---

2   See Elite 243, *Soviet State Security Forces 1917–46* for a detailed history; and see MAA 494, *World War II Soviet Armed Forces (1) 1939–41*, pp.41–44, for rank and insignia details.

A group of OGPU Internal Troops officers pose for the camera in 1924 wearing a variety of uniforms and civilian clothing. The pre-1917 greatcoats were easily transformed by the addition of the three 1922-regulation *razgovory* tabs across the right chest, and 'bastion'-topped rank tabs on the left forearm; here these, like the cap bands, all appear to be in branch colours and piping. The chest and sleeve tabs would begin to be phased out during 1924. (Author's collection)

Anti-guerrilla security troops of the OGPU in the field during the 1920s–30s. The standing men wear M1924 *'French'* tunics, the one sitting in the foreground what appears to be a heavyweight winter *gymnastiorka.* The officer at left, wearing a service cap and belt equipment with crossed braces, carries a US Thompson M1921 sub-machine gun. (Author's collection)

This resulted in a great extension of the labour camps, in mass arrests, legally sanctioned torture, rigged trials, and executions of innumerable victims – innumerable, because during the 'Great Terror' (1936–38) the imposition of most death sentences was devolved down the chain of authority as a merely administrative decision. From October 1936 executions without trial were sanctioned, and from spring 1937 the NKVD were given numerical targets for the numbers to be arrested.

The total number of arrests reached at least 1.4 million, and, according to the *'glasnost'*-era historians Okholin and Roginsky, the central records of the NKVD's GUGB security directorate alone list some 724,000 death sentences.

From January 1937 military tribunals were established (without the accused having the right to a defence), and from that May the armed forces were specifically targeted for purging. High-profile arrests and executions began in June 1937 with eight general officers, including Marshal Tukhachevsky. The sources give varying numbers of executions among the military, but among some 80,000 officers believed to have been serving in the Red Army and Navy the GUGB records list at least 41,000 death sentences handed down by military tribunals.

It is impossible to know how many officers simply disappeared, but, whatever the true number, the purge ripped the professional heart out of the Soviet armed forces' officer class. The arrests affected all echelons of command, the most numerous being of ranks from colonel down to company officers. However, amongst the highest ranks the ratio of victims was between 64 and 90 per cent: three of the five Marshals of the Soviet Union were executed, as were 434 of 684 general officers. These included 14 of 17 army commanders, 60 of 67 corps commanders, 136 of 199 divisional commanders, and 221 of 397 brigade commanders.

The inevitable effect of this beheading of the officer class was the loss of the most able, forward-looking, and therefore often outspoken men, while the unobtrusive and utterly obedient who never expressed an opinion had a better chance of surviving. Senior officers who survived for the time being naturally tried to keep a low profile, as it was dangerous to draw the attention of the NKVD for any reason.

Any officer, of whatever rank, who left the Soviet Union on military duties was in grave danger when he returned home. Many of the 3,000-odd advisors sent to help the Spanish Republicans during their civil war in 1936–39, and of the 3,600 sent to Nationalist China from October 1937, were shot when they returned, on suspicion of having been infected by such foreign contacts. The purges ended any positive influences from the armed forces of other nations, and crushed any initiative in the officer ranks.

Some recognition of these consequences may explain the unexpected release in autumn 1938 of about 15,000 imprisoned officers who had escaped execution, but one can easily imagine their submissive behaviour after being 're-habilitated' back to their units. Although the purges eased off in 1939, individual arrests continued until the eve of the German invasion in June 1941.

CAMPAIGNS IN THE 1930s

Far Eastern border clashes:
Changkufeng, 1938, and Khalkin Gol, 1939

During the 1930s border tensions arose in the Soviet Far East between the Red Army and the Japanese Kwantung Army, a semi-autonomous force occupying Japan's Manchurian proxy state, Manchukuo. The USSR had troops stationed in its own proxy Mongolian People's Republic, and both these client states also provided their sponsors with troops, mainly

The first five Marshals of the Soviet Union, created on 20 November 1935; Budenny and Blyucher stand behind (left to right) Tukhachevsky, Voroshilov and Yegorov. The 1937–38 military purges of Stalin's 'Great Terror' saw many of his oldest comrades subjected to arrest, torture, show trials, and execution as 'German agents' or 'Trotskyist counter-revolutionary conspirators'. Of these five marshals, the only two who survived were Budenny and Voroshilov; both were conservative-minded cavalrymen, while Tukachevsky had been an enthusiast for mechanization. Note the insignia of this new rank: a large gold star on red collar patches, and (centre foreground) a gold star above a broad gold and a narrower red chevron on both forearms. (Author's collection)

1939: three riflemen keeping watch over the steppe country on the border between Soviet-allied Mongolia and the Japanese puppet state of Manchukuo. They belong to the Soviet 57th Special Corps, the main Red Army formation in the region at the start of the conflict along the Khalkhin river. Just visible on their M1936 helmets are wide-mesh string nets for attaching grass camouflage. Among their field kit, all have the 'Lindemann' entrenching tool in a cloth cover on their right hips; the centre and right-hand men have gasmask satchels, and the aluminium water-bottle slung in a cloth cover. (Author's collection)

cavalry. Japan held that the border followed the Khalkhin Gol ('Khalka river'), while the Soviets claimed that it lay about 10 miles further east near the village of Nomonhan.

In July 1938 fighting broke out when troops of the RKKA's 39th Rifle Corps took the strategic Changkufeng heights close to Lake Khasan inside Manchukuo territory. They were challenged by the Japanese 19th Div, which pushed them back over the disputed border in a short but brutal two-day battle on 31 July–1 August.

The following summer, between mid-May and mid-September 1939, a much larger conflict took place along the Mongolian/Manchurian border. At its height this would involve some 74,000 Soviet and Mongolian troops, 550 tanks, 450 armoured cars and over 600 artillery pieces, plus 550 aircraft. The Japanese and their Manchukuo allies would field about 40,000 men with 90 tanks and tankettes, 300 guns and some 250 aircraft.

Early skirmishes, mainly between Mongolian and Manchukuo units, began in May 1939 along both banks of the Khalkin Gol. During June both sides brought up reinforcements, and on 5 June the up-and-coming *Komcor* (LtGen) Georgy Zhukov arrived to take command of the RKKA 57th Special Corps. He immediately demanded major reinforcements, but had only about 30,000 men by the end of that month, when Gen Komatsubara of the Japanese 23rd Div was ordered to attack.

A two-pronged Japanese offensive on 1–2 July sent the 23rd and part of 7th Div westwards across the river in the north, to drive Russian troops off heights on the west bank, and then swing southwards, aiming to meet the southern prong near Kawatama Bridge. Meanwhile, further south, Gen Masaomi's Yasuoka Detachment would attack RKKA positions on the east bank with about 90 AFVs and a few infantry battalions. The northern prong took its initial objectives and swung south, but was then almost encircled by Zhukov's bold committal of all his armour to a counterattack. Forced to fall back, it recrossed the river on 5 July. Meanwhile, on the east bank the Yasuoka Detachment failed, losing about half its armour, and after another Red Army counterattack on 9 July it was disbanded. A second major Japanese assault around Kawatama Bridge on 23–25 July also failed. By now Japanese casualties totalled about 5,000, and while Russian losses were higher, their level of motor transport allowed them to bring up men, ammunition and supplies much more easily.

By the time Zhukov struck back on 20 August, his command (now Soviet–Mongolian 1st Army Group) had a superiority of 1.5 to 1 in infantry, 2 to 1 in artillery, and, crucially, 4 to 1 in tanks. He launched his counter-offensive with 50,000 RKKA troops plus two Mongolian cavalry divisions, and 498 tanks, supported by 550 aircraft. The reinforced Japanese 23rd Div was outflanked and surrounded by two RKKA motorized rifle divisions, and when it tried to break out on 27 August it was virtually destroyed. Moscow and Tokyo agreed a ceasefire to take effect on 16 September.

Both sides' claimed casualty figures were unreliable, but subsequent research puts Soviet losses at just under 8,000 killed and 15,000-plus wounded (excluding 500–1,000 Mongolian casualties), with 253 tanks, 113 armoured cars and 250 aircraft knocked out. Kwantung Army records list about 8,600 Japanese dead and 9,000-plus wounded (excluding perhaps up to 3,000 Manchukuo casualties); they record 42 tanks knocked out, of which 29 were recovered, and total loss of 162 aircraft.

1939, Khalkin–Gol region: typical posed propaganda shot, supposedly showing two Red Army soldiers from separate units meeting on a recently captured hill. The *krasnoarmeyets* standing in front of the flag has long grass attached to his helmet. (Author's collection)

This was a major but costly victory over an inferior enemy, which would lead to a degree of overconfidence in the capabilities of the Red Army. On the other hand, it ensured Gen Zhukov's advancement; and it is believed to have helped persuade the Japanese high command towards a southern, rather than a western strategy on the eve of World War II.

Soviet invasion of Poland, September 1939

Both Germany and the Soviet Union had historical reasons for wanting to recover Polish territory which they considered to have been unjustly taken from them in the aftermath of World War I. German threats against Poland increased during 1939, and that country's fate was sealed on 23 August when a non-aggression pact was signed between the two powers, including a secret agreement over the division of Poland between them. Under the terms of this Ribbentrop–Molotov pact the USSR was to gain eastern Poland in return for remaining neutral when Germany invaded western and central Poland.

This German invasion started on 1 September, and while the outnumbered

Red Army artillerymen training during the build-up to the war with Finland in winter 1939. They are wearing felt overboots, and the fur–lined *bekesha* winter coat, which would not be issued to many soldiers during the Russo–Finnish War. The artillery piece is a 76.2mm M1909 mountain gun, an adaptation of the French 76mm which was made in Russia from 1909 to 1939, and was used by both sides in the 'Winter War'. (Author's collection)

Polish armed forces resisted desperately, the Red Army (its unwieldy official title now abbreviated to simply KA) gathered along the Russo–Polish border. Over two weeks the KA concentrated upwards of 25 rifle divisions, 16 cavalry divisions and 12 tank brigades, originally faced only by some 12,000 Polish border troops, of which some were transferred to resist the German invasion. Red Army soldiers were told that they were going to liberate the Polish people from a right-wing regime which had oppressed the working class since the state became independent in 1918. The KA crossed the border on 17 September, with strict orders not to confront the Wehrmacht advancing from the west. By the end of that day the Red Army had advanced 60 miles against the weakened Polish resistance. By the 21st, Russian troops reached the agreed demarcation line and halted, although a few mistaken clashes with German forward units did occur.

Almost immediately, NKVD units began transporting captured Polish Army officers and any civilian members of the educated classes who might offer a focus of resistance. Most of these 'class enemies' were never seen again, those who escaped summary execution being sent to the notorious Siberian labour camps.

The Russo-Finnish 'Winter War', 1939–40

Following the annexation of eastern Poland, Stalin pressed ahead with the expansion of Soviet territory in another region lost by Russia after the Revolution, since the Ribbentrop–Molotov pact had also given him a free hand on the Baltic. By October 1939 the three Baltic states – Estonia, Lithuania and Latvia – had been neutered by forced 'mutual assistance pacts' which allowed the installation of Soviet military bases (all three would be formally annexed to the USSR in August 1940).

Immediately, Stalin turned on Finland – a large, sparsely populated, but for 20 years staunchly independent republic. Finland's southernmost Karelian Isthmus, between the Gulf of Finland and Lake Ladoga, directly bordered Leningrad. In October 1939 Stalin used this, and the theoretical vulnerability of the nearby Soviet naval base at Kronstadt, as his pretexts for demanding unacceptable territorial concessions, which would have left Finland indefensible. Finland stalled for time while the C-in-C, Marshal Mannerheim, organized immediate mobilization. The talks broke down on 13 November; on the 26th a 'provocation' was engineered, when the Soviets claimed that Finnish artillery had shelled a border village; and on the 30th the Finnish capital, Helsinki, was bombed, and the Red Army began major offensives along Finland's northern, eastern and southern borders. Despite the huge disparity between the strengths of the armies committed – by 1 March 1940, about 760,600 Soviet troops to 346,000 Finnish – the resulting 'Winter War' would prove to be an acid test of the KA's readiness for modern international warfare.[3]

With a population of only 4 million, Finland had a regular army of about 33,000, expanded on mobilization of the territorial force to 127,800, with another 100,000 reservists available, plus up to 100,000 more mostly self-equipped paramilitary civil guards. The air force had just over 100 operational aircraft, many on the verge of obsolescence. The army had less than a dozen serviceable tanks, but its artillery fielded 500-plus guns in a variety of medium types, plus a few heavy guns and 100 mostly modern anti-tank guns.

The Red Army deployed five numbered armies along the roughly 500-mile Finnish–Soviet borders. In the far north were Fourteenth Army's 104th and 122nd Rifle Divisions. On the central front the Ninth Army had the 163rd, 44th and 54th Divs; further south, north of Lake Ladoga, was the Fifteenth Army with the 165th, 139th, 18th and 168th Divisions. In the far south, ready to strike Finland's main defensive lines across the Karelian Isthmus, was the Seventh Army, subsequently divided to add the separate Thirteenth Army; collectively, these comprised the 24th, 43rd, 70th, 123rd, and 49th, 90th, 142nd and 138th Rifle Divisions. In total, these infantry formations were initially supported by perhaps 2,500 tanks, though this figure would rise above 6,500 by the end of the war.

By late December 1939 the Finns were still holding out with difficulty in Karelia, but had made orderly retreats in face of the expected Soviet progress on other fronts. KA advances along rudimentary roads through snow-bound forest, in long columns hampered by armour and other vehicles, began to grind to a halt as they were pinned down and broken up by hit-and-run Finnish attacks led by fast-moving ski troops. On the central eastern front, in December 1939–January 1940, some 48,000 men of the KA's 163rd and elite 44th Rifle Divs, with 335 guns and 150 tanks and armoured

This log-revetted fire position in Finland, 1939–40, shows the conditions faced by both sides, but for which the Red Army was less well prepared; many men froze to death at their posts, partly because of a shortage of winter tents. These soldiers wear whatever warm clothing they can get hold of, including the standard woollen greatcoat. One rifleman has been issued a hooded white snow-camouflage coat, while the kneeling man, ready to pass a DP light machine gun magazine up to his comrade, wears his winter *budenovka* cap under his M1936 helmet. The shallow 'pan' magazines easily got damaged in action. (Getty Images/Sovfoto/170987611)

cars, were caught in a gigantic trap around the town of Suomussalmi. Before long their command-and-control was breaking down, and units which became isolated were disintegrating under all-round attacks. Many of the often poorly-clothed and ill-supplied soldiers simply froze to death at their posts overnight, and only small numbers eventually escaped the encirclements, abandoning much equipment.

By the end of December, after a month of fighting, five of the Red Army's six separate advances had largely failed, their only success being in the far north in the relative sideshow of the Murmansk front. As exhausted units withdrew from the front lines, on 7 January Gen Semyon Timoshenko was appointed to command the KA's North-West Group of Forces, and spent the following weeks preparing for an all-out offensive to break the dogged Finnish resistance in Karelia. This greatly strengthened effort, launched across the ice of Viipuri (Vyborg) Bay on 1 February, would involve 460,000 men with 3,000 tanks, 3,350 guns and 1,300 aircraft, faced by about 150,000 exhausted Finns clinging to what was left of the Mannerheim Line defences. On 12 February the USSR offered to negotiate through Swedish intermediaries, but fierce fighting continued until 27 February, when the Finns were forced back into their final defences. A peace treaty was signed on 12 March; Stalin's terms were brutal, costing Finland 10 per cent of its national territory including Karelia, and displacing some 450,000 citizens. However, Finland's brave and astonishingly effective resistance had secured the nation's continuing independent existence.

The 'Winter War' had cost the KA some 200,000 dead and 123,000 wounded (against about 70,000 Finnish casualties), and its unwelcome

1939–41: a crowd of Red Army and Air Force personnel on an airstrip gathered around an officer reading them through an article in a Soviet newspaper – perhaps *Pravda*? They wear a variety of uniforms and headgear. The Air Force men (left, and centre background) have the dark blue *pilotka* sidecap, piped for officers with light blue; they also have dark fleece-lined coats, and one of them the *shapka-ushanka* fleece cap. One soldier (centre right background) wears the padded leather crash helmet of the armoured troops, while the others wear either the khaki *pilotka* or the old *budenovka*. (Author's collection)

lessons made even Stalin reflect on the reasons behind the failures of the complacent but purge-weakened Red Army. In April 1940 he was quoted as saying: 'The cult of the Revolutionary War and the experience of the Civil War are proving to be obstacles to progress in bringing the Red Army up to date' – as near as he could come to a public admission of the damage he had caused. He was shocked by the army's poor performance, and began to doubt the ability of his favourites. In May 1940, Marshal Voroshilov was replaced as Commissar of Defence by Marshal Timoshenko.

The Red Army in 1941

In late 1940 the Red Army was spread far and wide facing actual or perceived enemies along all of the USSR's extensive borders. It had 34 rifle and 8 cavalry divisions watching the Imperial Japanese Army in Manchuria. There were 15 rifle divisions facing Finland; 18–20 in newly-occupied Estonia, Latvia and Lithuania, and 22 divisions occupying eastern Poland. Other forces available totalled 90 rifle divisions, 23 cavalry divisions and 28 mechanized brigades.

It is well-documented that the unpreparedness of the KA to meet the shock of the German attack on the Soviet Union on 22 June 1941 was partly due to Stalin's refusal to believe the many warnings provided by his intelligence services in both the East and the West. It was not until the early hours of Sunday 22 June that he finally ordered a vaguely-worded warning to be given to front-line commanders. This was too imprecise and far too late to make any difference. Hours later the western borders were struck by some 3,200,000 German and German-allied troops in 148 divisions, with 3,550 tanks and 7,184 artillery pieces, backed by 2,000 aircraft.

Facing them were 170 Red Army divisions, reportedly enjoying a superiority of 7 to 1 in tank numbers and 4 to 1 in aircraft. However, many of the formations in the West had never been fully formed, and are believed to have had a shortfall totalling about 1.5 million men. Crucially, they were also demoralized. Since the purges many formations had been under-officered; the officers graduated since 1938 had received shortened and inadequate training, and nearly all were too cowed to show any initiative in the face of unexpected attack, while senior ranks refused to take responsibility for decisions. Although more modern designs were just coming into service, most of the KA's tanks and aircraft were technically inferior to those of the Wehrmacht, and their numerical superiority was quickly nullified by the speed, shock and focus of the German attacks. Within hours the Army Air Force in the border regions had been virtually destroyed on the ground. This cleared the skies for the Luftwaffe to deliver relentless close support to the mechanized divisions that were soon advancing at pace, cutting through the initial resistance to begin enormous encircling movements on the central and southern fronts.[4]

UNIFORMS, 1922–41

The Tsarist army had fought World War I uniformed mainly in shades of khaki, with grey greatcoats. Due to its inevitably very uneven and

---

4   See Campaign series 129, 148 & 186, *Operation Barbarossa 1941 (1) Army Group South, (2) Army Group North,* and *(3) Army Group Centre.*

Seen at a Party sports meeting in October 1923, about a year before they both lost their posts in the power-struggle following Lenin's death, are the Moscow Military District commander N.I. Muralov (left) and the Commissar for Military and Naval Affairs, Leon Trotsky. Their *budenovka* caps are of winter weight, but have the front peak and rear neck flap cut as on the 1922 summer-weight version. Both are wearing the new *kaftan* greatcoat with coloured collar patches and the chest tabs introduced in 1919 (Trotsky's coat seems to be made of civilian material with a noticeable 'pile'.). As a Trotsky loyalist, Muralov would be executed in January 1937 during Stalin's purges, and Trotsky would be assassinated in exile in Mexico in August 1940. (Author's collection)

patchy logistics, the Red Army emerged from the Civil War in 1922 wearing a wide variety of whatever clothing was regionally available. The majority of soldiers had khaki uniforms (in the British usage of the term – drab brown/olive) from pre-1917 Imperial Army stocks, or various others supplied to the Tsarist and White armies by the Entente powers during World War I and the Civil War. Over the next 19 years Red Army uniforms would be gradually standardized and developed, culminating in a range of modern orders-of-dress in the mid-1930s. This was again an inconsistent process, due to widely dispersed manufacture, and to the inevitably long delays in compliance with any given set of regulations over the whole area of the USSR.[5]

Headgear

The best-known type of field headgear worn in 1922 was a cloth *shlem* ('helmet') type. Actually designed in 1913, reportedly by Viktor Vasnatsov, but not issued to the Imperial Army, this was adopted in January 1919 by the Bolshevik RMSR (Revolutionary Military Council). In widespread use from early 1920, it had several names, including *bogatirka* – recalling the 'spired' helmets worn by some medieval Russian warriors – but it became universally known as the *budenovka*, after the Red Cavalry commander Semyon Budenny (see Plates A1 & A2). Cheap to produce from available materials, it was locally made in slightly differing versions, but it was characterized by

---

5   The beginning and end of this journey will be found described and illustrated in more detail in MAA 293, *The Russian Civil War (1) The Red Army*, and MAA 464, *World War II Soviet Armed Forces (1) 1939–41*.

the crown rising to a point, which made Bolshevik troops easier to identify in Civil War battles when both sides wore very similar clothing. Regulation winter and summer patterns appeared in January 1922. The former, of dark grey woollen cloth, had a cloth peak (visor) and a button-up ear-and-neck flap; the latter, in khaki cotton, had the peak and a smaller permanent rear neck flap made in one piece. Slightly modified in 1927, it remained in field use right up until 1941; the M1927 was dark grey for officers, mid-grey for enlisted ranks. On all versions the universal M1922 red-enamelled or painted star badge, with the hammer-&-sickle motif, was pinned to a 95mm branch-colour cloth star backing. A floppy-brimmed khaki *'panama'* sunhat was also used in Central Asia in the 1920–30s (see F1), and became general issue for hot-region service in 1938.

Versions of the Imperial Army's stiff-peaked (visored) M1910 service cap (*furashka*) were widely worn throughout and after the Civil War, those in use in the 1920s usually being termed the M1919 or M1922. From 1924 they were authorized for officers in summer, beside the winter-weight *budenovka* worn in cold weather. Between 1924 and 1935 officially, and until 1939 in practice, enlisted ranks wore soft-crowned service caps (with card stiffeners only for the band and visor). These were usually plain khaki, and of a smarter model from 1928 (see D1).

However, some categories of personnel had distinctive coloured crowns and bands – notably, OGPU/NKVD security forces (see B2), though not universally, and some photographs show them in khaki caps. Initially the RKKA's cavalry enjoyed elite status, and from 1924 the

A Red Army unit commander on parade with his troops in winter 1922/23. As a common 1920s–30s alternative to the *budenovka* he wears a pre-Revolution style astrakhan *papakha* cap, here lacking the usual red star badge. This photograph shows the vertical 'slash' chest and waist pockets of the 1919 *kaftan*. Under magnification the collar patches, chest tabs, and left forearm rank tab of 1922 regulations can all be made out, but in plain coat-cloth for lack of coloured material. Note the metal RKKA badge worn on the cross-strap. (Author's collection)

Desert troops of the Red Army somewhere in Soviet Central Asia in 1937, wearing the khaki service cap as field headgear; that of the officer (left) is more stiffened than those of his soldiers. The central man is a locally-recruited Turkic interpreter. (Author's collection)

cavalry divisions and their constituent regiments were distinguished in this way; see accompanying Table 1.

Table 1: Cavalry service cap colours, 1924–29
The 11th–3rd, 7th, and 9th–11th Cav Divs each had four cavalry regiments, plus HQ and artillery elements; the 10th Cav Div, five cavalry regiments; and the 4th–6th & 8th Cav Divs, six cavalry regiments. In all divisions the HQ wore dark blue cap bands, and the artillery regiment black bands.
1st Cav Div: crowns lime-green, piped black; *bands* red (1st Regt), mid-green (2nd), yellow (3rd), white (4th)
2nd Cav Div: crowns mid-green, piped yellow; *bands* 7th–10th Regts, as 1st Div units
3rd Cav Div: crowns yellow, piped lime-green; *bands* 13th–16th Regts, as 1st Div units
4th Cav Div: crowns dull red, piped yellow; *bands* 19th–22nd Regts, as 1st Div units; plus 23rd Regt blue, 24th Regt orange.
5th Cav Div: crowns red, piped dark blue; *bands* 25th–30th Regts, as 4th Div units
6th Cav Div: crowns dark green, piped yellow; *bands* 31st–36th Regts, as 4th Div units
7th Cav Div: crowns mid-blue, piped white; *bands* 37th–40th Regts, as 1st Div units
8th Cav Div: crowns dark red, piped black; *bands* 43rd–48th Regts, as 4th Div units
9th Cav Div: crowns orange, piped black; *bands* 49th–52nd Regts, as 1st Div units
10th Cav Div: crowns light blue , piped white; *bands* 55th–59th Regts, as first units in 4th Div
11th Cav Div: crowns dark blue, piped yellow: *bands* 67th, 69th, 88th & 90th Regts, as 1st Div units.
In addition, there were eight non-divisional, three-regiment cavalry brigades, in which regimental band colours were in the same sequence as the first three units in 1st–3rd Cav Divs, and the crowns in plain colours, unpiped, as follows:
1st Bde dark blue; *2nd Bde* mid-green; *4th Bde* dark red; *5th Bde* red; *6th Bde* dark green; *7th Bde* mid-blue; *8th Bde* crimson; *9th Bde* orange.

Army field telephone operator, wearing the khaki *pilotka* cap which was widely introduced under the December 1935 regulations to replace both the lightweight *budenovka* and the peaked service cap as service and summer field headgear. It bears the universal M1922 metal red star badge (Author's collection)

As the Red Army strove to streamline its uniform supply these complex regimental caps were deemed to be an expensive luxury, and by 1929 they were phased out. Henceforward all cavalry caps had khaki crowns and blue bands, and photographs show that these remained in service into World War II. When Cossack units were reinstated after 1936 they wore their traditional black fleece caps: for the Don host, a taller *papakha* with a red top, and for the Kuban and Terek Cossacks a lower *kubanka*, with red and light blue tops respectively. (They also received complex traditional uniforms for parade dress.)

Under the comprehensive dress regulations of December 1935, a new service cap, its use limited to officers and senior (i.e. re-enlisted) NCO ranks, had a khaki crown with band and piping in branch colours. Exceptions included two branches which received complete new coloured service uniforms: the armoured troops, which had light 'steel-grey' cap crowns with black bands and red piping, and the Army Air Force, in dark blue with light blue piping. NKVD security and internal troops continued to wear caps with dark blue crowns, dull red bands and raspberry-red piping, and the Frontier Troops bright green crowns, black bands and bright red piping.

Also in 1935, a khaki sidecap (in US usage, 'overseas' or 'garrison' cap) was introduced as summer field and service headgear for all

(continued on page 33)

1922–1924
1: *Zamkomvzvoda*, Rifles, 1922
2: Machine-gunner, Rifles, 1923
3: Troop commander, 3rd Cav Regt, 1924

1923–1929
1: Border guard, OGPU Frontier Troops, 1923
2: Junior commander, OGPU Internal Troops, 1927
3: LMG-gunner, Rifles; Manchuria, winter 1928/29
4: *Komvzvoda*, 23rd Cav Regt, 4th Cav Div, 1928

B

COUNTER-INSURGENCY, 1920s–30s
1: Light machine-gunner, Rifles; Fergana Valley, 1927
2: Tajik auxiliary, 1927
3: Border guard, OGPU Frontier Troops; Central Asia, 1930

C

1932–38
1: *Krasnoarmeyets,* Rifles, 1932
2: *Kapitan*, Artillery, 1935–36
3: Motorcyclist, Armoured Troops, 1938

D

1936–40
1: Light machine-gunner, Rifles, 1940
2: *Otdelyonniy Komandir*, T-27 unit, 1936
3: Company *politruk*, Rifles, 1938

E

SOVIET FAR EAST, 1938–39
1: *Leytenant,* Artillery, 32nd Rifle Div, 1938
2: *Komkor* G.K. Zhukov, 1939
3: *Otdelyonnly Komandir,* 82nd Rifle Regt; 1939

F

POLAND & BALTIC STATES, 1939–40
1: Militiaman; Baltic States, 1940
2: Border guard, NKVD Frontier Troops; Poland, 1939
3: *Kapitan*, Armoured Troops; Poland, 1939

G

THE 'WINTER WAR', 1939–40
1: *Krasnoarmeyets,* 44th Rifle Div, 1940
2: *Major*, Engineers, 1939
3: Ski scout, 1940
4: Volunteer, 'Finnish People's Army', 1940

Soviet cavalrymen (note the sabres) serving in Central Asia in the early 1930s, and wearing the 'panama' sunhat that would become regulation issue in 1938. At right, note field shirt in dark khaki and trousers in light summer khaki. In the far-flung regions of the Soviet Union hunting was a favourite pastime, especially for officers. The kill here is a Siberian or Amur tiger – today a seriously endangered species – whose skin would have made an impressive trophy for an officer when he returned home. (Author's collection)

ranks (see E3), although its introduction was gradual. Called the *pilotka*, because it was originally Air Force issue, from 1936 the sidecap was adopted by all branches of the RKKA to replace the summer *budenovka* and the enlisted ranks' service cap. For officers it had a small branch-colour badge-backing for the M1922 red star, and branch-colour piping on the crown and turn-up flap edges. (Both these were officially discontinued from January 1941.) In the armoured branch and the Army Air Force it was made in steel-grey, piped red, and dark blue, piped light blue, respectively.

Various winter fur and fleece hats were worn at need throughout the interwar period (see B3), and many officers wore astrakhan lambswool caps of varying shape and quality. The first official-issue *shapka-ushanka* (see H4) was not introduced until 1940, to replace the winter *budenovka* for all ranks. It was of grey cloth, with real (for officers) or false (for enlisted men) lambswool fleece lining on the turn-up front and ear/neck flaps.

Helmets

Like the rest of their equipment, in the 1920s the Red Army's steel helmets came from Imperial Army stores. In 1916 the Tsarist army had introduced a version of the French Adrian M1915, though it was not widely issued. During the Civil War limited numbers were used by both sides, and from 1922 by the Red Army (see D3 and E1), some being manufactured using machinery imported from France in World War I. Another World War I model, with a ventilator at the apex instead of the Adrian's 'comb', had been made in Finland while that country was still part of the Russian Empire, and small numbers

1936: good study of a DP light machine-gunner wearing the Adrian helmet; note the red-painted star plate standing proud at the front. He wears his greatcoat in a 'horseshoe' roll over his left shoulder. The dark collar patches with light piping suggest one of the technical branches, such as the artillery or engineers. (Author's collection)

1939: staged photograph of Soviet soldiers being greeted as 'liberators' in one of the Baltic states. They wear new M1939 steel helmets, which differed externally from the subsequent M1940 only in the placing of rivets. (Author's colletion)

continued in service throughout the 1920s and 1930s (see D2). In 1941 the Adrian was still sometimes seen, alongside the heavier M1936 helmet (see F3 and H1) with its flared 'Swiss-type' brim and a small comb. While this had been intended to replace all earlier models, on the eve of World War II the M1936 itself began to be replaced with simplified M1939 and M1940 patterns with reduced brims. Armoured crews and motorcycle troops wore padded black leather or later canvas crash helmets, which came in several models. (see E2 and G3).

1939: the corporal commander of a T-26 light tank. He wears goggles on the M1933 leather crash helmet, M1935 dark blue overalls, and leather gauntlets, and has binoculars slung from his neck. The overalls seem to have come in both double- and single-breasted versions, both with fly fronts. The greatcoat collar patches attached to them are in black with red upper edge piping, and bear the two triangles of an *otdelyonniy komandir.* (Author's collection)

Field and service uniforms

In the aftermath of the Civil War some use was still made of ex-Imperial Army tunics. However, for all ranks by far the most common upper garment from 1922 was the traditional Russian pull-over field shirt (*gymnastiorka)*, hanging untucked over the thighs and with buttoned cuff bands. The 1919 pattern had a low standing collar, and two exposed or concealed buttons down a chest placket; the collar was sometimes fastened centrally, sometimes with a tab off-set to one side. The M1922 *gymnastiorka* had a fall collar and two breast pockets, and was made in winter and summer weights. Some also had concealed slash waist pockets, and some 'commanders' wore versions tailored in superior cloth. The 1922 regulations specified dark grey for winter and light grey for summer, but in fact colours always varied, many being khaki/olive drab (*zashchitniy tsvet*) in winter and sand-khaki in summer.

To distinguish Red Army troops from the Whites during the Civil War, from April 1919 three 'bastion-ended' cloth tabs (*razgovory)* in the wearer's branch colour were sewn to the chest of the field shirt and greatcoat (see B1), sometimes with the top one on the field shirt's standing collar (see A1). These tabs were ordered discontinued from 1924. After 1935 officers' field shirts acquired branch-colour piping to the collar and cuff tops, any waist pockets disappeared, and collars were adapted to accommodate the new rank patches introduced from December that year.

Smartly turned-out Red Army men, apparently singing or chanting while parading on May Day 1928. Their uniforms are standard for the late 1920s: the dark khaki service cap, **gymnastiorka** and trousers, with polished *sapogi* boots, plus belt equipment and rolled grey greatcoat. It is difficult to identify the metal collar-patch branch symbol of the left-hand NCO, and the soldier ahead of him seems to display only a corporal's two triangles. (Author's collection)

The 1924 dress regulations saw the introduction, for 'commanders' including senior NCOs, of a new four-pocket service tunic (see B2 & B4) to be worn alongside their continuing use of the *gymnastiorka*. Popularly known, like its Tsarist forerunner, as the '*French*', this had five front buttons, and appeared with varying pocket details. Some had pleated patch breast pockets and internal waist pockets, all with external buttoned flaps, but some had internal breast pockets. Some tunics were made from heavier fabric and were intended to be worn without greatcoats. The design of the M1924 tunic changed slightly over the years, and a wholly new version was introduced as part of the December 1935 dress regulations.

This six-button M1935 tunic had pleated patch breast pockets and internal waist pockets, with external buttoned flaps. It was piped in branch colours around the fall collar and the top of the straight cuffs. Officers of the armoured branch wore the service uniform in 'steel grey' rather than khaki, and of the Air Force in dark blue, and both wore the tunic collar pressed open over a white shirt and black necktie.

Legwear and footwear

The main type of trousers worn by the Red Army throughout the 1920s and 1930s were known by the traditional term *sharovari*. For officers these might be genuine breeches, but for enlisted ranks they were cut as 'semi-breeches', flared in the thigh and tapered down to below the knee. Cavalry trousers often had reinforcement on the inner leg, and from February 1941

Troops on the march in summer 1928 wearing sand-khaki lightweight uniforms, but note variations in shades. While the troops wear puttees and ankle boots, the officers and senior NCOs on the flank of the column have high boots. (Author's collection)

all troops received trousers with reinforcement on the knees. Most trousers were in drab khaki wool, though during the 1920s lighter khaki cotton versions might be seen in summer. Dark blue breeches were worn by 'commanders' of mounted branches and by the OGPU/NKVD, including its Frontier Troops, and after 1935 could be worn by all officers with service dress; they were normally piped down the outseam in branch colours. Straight khaki trousers were introduced for officers from 1935 as undress or 'walking-out' uniform. Some photographs also show enlisted men of cavalry and other branches wearing dark blue trousers for parade dress.

The most common footwear for all ranks were traditional black leather calf-length boots *(sapogi)*, though in the 1920s commanders and commissars often had superior privately-purchased riding boots. There were frequent shortages of leather, so troops were often issued brown leather ankle boots instead, worn with khaki woollen puttees (see A2 & D1). Protective winter footwear included felt overboots *(valenki)*, but these were held in unit stores and often in short supply. Some composite winter boots of leather and felt construction were also available, but are seldom seen in photographs other than of higher-ranking officers.

Greatcoats and protective clothing

Throughout our period the usual cold-weather uniform in all orders-of-dress included the double-breasted woollen greatcoat *(shinel,* or in 1919 *kaftan),* with a deep turn-down collar and turn-up cuffs. Although some examples of collars, cuffs and even pocket flaps in contrasting colours and/or with branch-colour piping were initially seen, the greatcoat generally altered little over time apart from its applied insignia. Longer patterns with deeper rear vents were issued to the cavalry. Coats normally fastened with concealed hooks or buttons down the right side, though the 1919 and 1922 uniforms, which featured the branch-colour *razgovory* chest tabs, often had exposed buttons. The colour varied markedly over time and place; in 1919 it was specified as khaki, in 1922 as grey; from 1927 as dark grey for 'commanders' and mid-grey for enlisted ranks; and in August 1941 as khaki again. In practice, examples might appear in any shade from grey, through brownish-grey, to khaki. The officers'

M1935 had two rows of six exposed brass buttons, and for general officers extensive edge-piping (in red for marshals and army generals, in branch colours for the more junior grades).

In the field, some motorcyclists and armoured vehicle commanders wore black leather coats or jackets from at least 1925. Later an M1929 black leather three-quarter length double-breasted jacket (see G3) was issued, and subsequently M1935 dark blue 'moleskin' fabric equivalents. By the eve of World War II the leather jackets began to be replaced with cheaper proofed canvas. All armour crews had dark blue or black M1935 overalls.

Throughout the interwar period some kind of locally-made sheepskin winter watchcoat might be acquired at need (see B3), but a new fur-lined, double-breasted *bekesha* was officially introduced in 1931 (see H2). The pale khaki-drab quilted cotton winter overjacket *(telogreika)* is called the M1938 in some sources, but it was reportedly during the 'Winter War' that it was first issued to some troops (see H1) for lack of greatcoats.

Rank and insignia
A decree by Lenin on 16 December 1917 abolished all ranks and insignia of the Imperial Army. (The *pogoni* shoulder boards, in particular, were rejected as a symbol of the supposedly aristocratic officer class.) During 1918 the tactical leaders of the irregular Bolshevik Red Guards, and the Red Army that replaced them, were initially elected by their comrades, and were distinguished largely by red field-signs added to clothing and headgear in the form of armbands, ribbon stripes or rosettes.

This detail from a larger group photograph of 1923 shows officers ('commanders') wearing greatcoats. These mainly display the 1922 branch-colour collar patches, chest tabs in branch colours or plain cloth, and the left-forearm rank tab. Despite his youth, the man in the right foreground shows the red star over four red squares that identified a regimental commander or deputy commander, or the commander of a detached battalion. (Author's collection)

This was obviously inefficient, and in January 1919 a new system was authorized. 'Officers' as a separate caste would be replaced by a more egalitarian sequence of 'commanders', with abbreviated titles referring to their command appointment. These functions were identified by cloth insignia sewn to the left forearm, all surmounted by a single red star badge. (Commissars would wear a red sleeve star only.) There was some variation at first, but eventually the abbreviated command titles and insignia were adopted much as in the accompanying Table 2.

Table 2: Command titles & insignia, 16 January 1919

(From the most senior downwards:)
Kommanduyushiy Frontom = Front commander (4 diamond shapes)
Komandarm = Army cdr (3 diamonds)
Nachdiv or *Komdiv* = Division cdr (2 diamonds)
Kombrig = Brigade cdr (1 diamond)
Kompolka = Regimental cdr (4 squares)
Kombat = Battalion cdr (3 squares)
Komroty = Company cdr (2 squares)
Komvzvoda = Platoon cdr (1 square)
Starshina = Sergeant-major equivalent (3 triangles)
Pomkomvzvoda or *Zamkomvzvoda* = Deputy ptn cdr (2 triangles)
Komandir Otdeleniya = Section cdr (1 triangle).
Krasnoarmeyets = 'Red Army man' = private (red star only)

New regulations in January 1922 placed the left-forearm star and appointment symbols on a 'bastion'-topped vertical tab in branch colours and piping (see example, Plate A3), though if colours were not available

These troops seen on parade in Red Square in May 1925 are motorcyclists of a transport unit, wearing Adrian M1916 helmets from former Imperial Army stocks. Even at this early date they have also been issued with four-pocket three-quarter length leather jackets, resembling those later worn by RKKA armoured vehicle commanders. (Author's collection)

plain uniform cloth was used (see A2). In June 1924 the triangle, square and diamond symbols were ordered repeated on rectangular patches, of the branch-of-service colours and piping, on the collar of the *gymnastiorka* and the *French* tunic. These, and the lozenge-shaped piped branch-colour collar patches already seen on the greatcoat, often also displayed unit identification.

By regulations of 22 September and 3 December 1935 the Red Army abandoned the '*komandiri*' categories for appointments below *kombrig*, and re-introduced conventional ranks for field and company officers, though not yet for generals. Two classes of *komandarm* and a new rank of *marshal* were introduced. The gold-edged red metal 'jewels' of the rank insignia were still to be worn on the rectangular branch-colour patches on the collars of the *gymnastiorka* (see F1) and the tunic, and on the lozenge-shaped branch-colour patches on the greatcoat collar. These patches were piped in gold for officers, and in branch colours for enlisted ranks. For the most senior ranks large collar and sleeve stars were elaborately embroidered in gold on red. For officers of combat branches (but not supporting services), new additional rank insignia were now to be worn on both forearms, in the form of gold and red downwards-pointing chevrons of varying thickness (see F2). The new hierarchy was as the accompanying Table 3; however, regulations of July 1940 would revise this sequence considerably, as in Table 4.

This officer photographed in 1936 wears a peaked service cap and four-pocket *French* tunic following 1935 regulations, but apparently made from lighter-weight cloth than normal. The cap's visor and band have been stiffened with lines of stitching in place of or, in addition to, the normal card inserts. Another odd point is that he still wears the red star badge 'point down', as seen during 1918 but not officially thereafter. The four square red 'jewels' on his collar patches are an example of the complications to the sequence sometimes seen. They identify a *starshiy leytenant – 1go ranga*, or 'senior lieutenant, first rank'. The insignia of senior lieutenant was three squares; but if two officers of the same rank were serving together within a sub-unit, the more senior displayed four squares. (Author's collection)

Table 3: Command titles & insignia, 3 December 1935
(From most senior downwards (collar insignia/cuff insignia & chevrons)
Chief commanders:
Marshal Sovetskogo Soyuza (50mm gold star/50mm star + 30mm gold & 15mm red chevrons)
Komandarm 1-go ranga (22mm star + 4 diamonds/50mm star + 30mm gold)
Komandarm 2-go ranga (4 diamonds/4 x 15mm gold)
Komkor (3 diamonds/3 x 15mm gold)
Komdiv (2 diamonds/2 x 15mm gold)
Kombrig (1 diamond/1 x 15mm gold)
Senior commanders:
Polkovnik = Colonel (3 vertical bars/15mm gold, red, gold)
Major (2 bars/2 x 15mm red)
Kapitan (1 bar/1 x 15mm red}
Intermediate commanders:
Starshiy Leytenant (3 squares/3 x 7.5mm red)
Leytenant (2 squares/2 x 7.5mm red)
Mladshiy Leytenant (from Aug 1937: 1 square/1 x 7.5mm red)
Junior commanders:
Starshina (Sgt major; 4 triangles)
Mladshiy Komvzvod (Sergeant; 3 triangles)
Otdelyonniy Komandir (Corporal; 2 triangles)
Krasnoarmeyets (Private; no rank insignia)

Table 4: Command titles & insignia, 13 July 1940 *et seq*

General officers' titles & insignia, 13 July 1940; field & company officers', 26 July; enlisted ranks' titles, 2 November; enlisted insignia, 1 January 1941).

From most senior downwards (collar insignia/cuff insignia & chevrons)

Chief commanders:

Marshal Sovetskogo Soyuza (50mm star + gold leaves/star, + on red backing: 15mm gold, gold leaves, 15mm gold chevrons)

General Armiyii (5 gold stars/star + 15mm red, 30mm gold, 7.5mm red)

General-Polkovnik (Colonel-general; 4 stars/ star + 30mm gold, 7.5mm red)

General-Leytenant (3 stars/star + 30mm gold, 7.5mm red)

General-Mayor (2 stars/star + 30mm gold, 7.5mm red)

Senior commanders:

Polkovnik (4 bars/on red backing, 2 x 7.5mm, 1 x 15mm gold)

Podpoulkovnik (Lt Colonel; 3 bars/on red backing, 1 x 7.5mm, 1 x 15mm gold)

Mayor (2 bars/chevrons as LtCol)

Kapitan (1 bar/on red backing, 2 x 7.5mm, 1 x 15mm gold)

Intermediate commanders:

Starshiy Leytenant (3 squares/on red backing, 3 x 7.5mm gold)

Leytenant (2 squares/on red backing, 2 x 7.5mm gold)

Mladshiy Leytenant (1 square/on red backing, 1 x 7.5mm gold)

Junor commanders:

Starshina (1 large, 4 small triangles)

Starshiy Serzhant (1 large, 3 small triangles)

Serzhant (1 large, 2 small triangles)

Mladshiy Serzhant (1 large, 1 small triangles)

Privates:

Yefreytor (1 large triangle)

Krasnoarmeyets (no rank insignia)

(*Note:* NCOs' collar patches bore, from the rear forwards, the large triangle in the upper rear corner, then a branch symbol, then the small triangles.)

Three young soldiers of the Railway Troops pose for a studio shot in 1936; they still wear the service cap rather than the new sidecap. Their collar patches are black, piped with royal blue, and bear the branch symbol introduced in 1924, which features (oddly) a crossed axe and anchor; ahead of this is the regimental number '5'. Some branch symbols were altered during 1936, but not this example. While two of these men wear the standard khaki *gymnastiorka,* their comrade sports a lightweight white summer undress ('walking-out') version. For all ranks such garments were not regulation, but tolerated private purchases. (Author's collection)

Branch colours

Those initially adopted in January 1919 were as follows: infantry ('rifles'), raspberry-red (crimson); cavalry, blue; artillery, orange;

engineers, black; air force, light blue; and frontier troops, bright green. These were displayed on lozenge-shaped greatcoat collar patches, and, from January 1922, on field shirts. These new rectangular collar patches were piped on three edges in black for all except black patches, and red for black patches. The artillery facing now became black with red piping. However, most of the new 'bastion'-topped left-sleeve rank tabs were piped red. In June 1923, the piping of these and the *razgovory* chest tabs was standardized to match that on collar patches.

Over time a number of new branches and services were introduced, each with its own combination of collar patch and piping colours. The sequence for the major branches and services confirmed by the December 1935/March 1936 regulations was as Table 5.

Table 5: Branch colours, 10 March 1936		
Branch	*Colour*	*Enlisted ranks' piping*
Infantry	Raspberry-red	Black
Cavalry	Blue	Black
Armoured	Black	Red
Motorcycle (1940)	Black	Red
Artillery	Black	Red
Engineers, Transport, Railway & Signals	Black	Royal blue
Chemical	Black	Black
Air Force & Paratroops	Light blue	Light blue
Supply, Admin, & Medical services	Dark green	Red
(*Note:* Officers' collar-patch piping = gold in combat branches, and matching enlisted ranks in services. Officers' piping on caps, collars & cuffs in main branch colour.)		

Branch insignia

These appeared in two types: cloth sleeve patches, and metal collar-patch symbols.

Between 1918 and 1920 a number of non-regulation branch and unit patches began to proliferate on the left upper sleeves of coats and field shirts. During January–April 1920, patches were regularized for the major combat branches (rifles, cavalry, artillery and engineers). Typically, these were in branch colours, of square, diamond or 'horseshoe' shape, and

1932: Red Cross officers and volunteers photographed during a civil defence exercise in Central Asia. Note the differing shapes of the service caps. The Geneva Cross symbol is repeated in red on a white disc on the collar patches of the female volunteers. The man at right may perhaps display the dark green branch colour, piped red, of the Medical Service, but has no branch symbol or rank insignia. (Author's collection)

bearing a branch symbol and red star against a sunburst motif. Larger red patches were awarded to units which had distinguished themselves, bearing the word *obraztsovy* ('exemplary') in yellow at the top. Such patches were further formalized under the January 1922 regulations, but discontinued from 1924.

During 1922–24, white metal branch symbols began to appear on field shirt, tunic and greatcoat collar patches, initially behind/above unit numbers and later in combination with the geometric rank symbols. Many others were added and/or discontinued over the years. However, the infantry ('rifles') had no symbol until 1940, being considered as the 'default' branch of service. The symbols listed in June 1924 regulations were replaced in March 1936 by brass symbols, of which the major examples were as follows:

Infantry (from July 1940): Crossed rifles on target
Cavalry: Crossed sabres on horseshoe
Armoured: A tank in profile (see Plate G3a)
Artillery: Crossed cannon barrels
Engineers: Crossed axes (plus several speciality variations)
Signals: Red star, wings & lightning bolts
Air Force & Paratroops: Winged two-blade propellor
Medical service: Chalice & snake.

SELECT BIBLIOGRAPHY

Benevenuti, Francesco, *The Bolsheviks and the Red Army 1918–1922* (CUP Archive, 1988)

Erickson, John, *The Soviet High Command 1918–1941* (Macmillan & Co Ltd, 1962)

Jowett, Philip, & Snodgrass, Brent, *Finland at War 1939–45*, Elite 141 (Osprey, 2006)

Minz, I., *The Red Army* (New York International Publishers, 1943)

Moynahan, Brian, *The Claws of the Bear – A History of the Soviet Armed Forces from 1917 to the Present* (Hutchinson, 1989)

Okholin, N.G. & Roginsky, A.B., eds, *The Great Terror*, 2 vols (Memorial, Moscow, 1991–92/2007)

Reese, Roger R., *Stalin's Reluctant Soldiers, A Social History of the Red Army 1925–1941* (University Press of Kansas, 1996)

Reese, Roger R., *The Soviet Military Experience: A History of the Soviet Army, 1918–1991* (Routledge, 2000)

Seaton, Albert & Joan, *The Soviet Army 1918 to the Present* (Bodley Head, 1986)

Shalito, A., Savchenkov, I., Roginsky, N. & Tsyplenkov, K., *Red Army Uniforms 1918–1945 in Color Photographs* (Tekhnika Molodyozi, 1999)

Shalito, A., Savcheko, I., Mollo, A., photos Kozlov, A. & Pyskarov, I., *Red Army Uniforms of World War II in Colour Photographs* (Windrow & Greene, 1993)

Webster, David & Nelson, Chris, *Uniforms of the Soviet Union 1918–1945* (Schiffer Military History, Atglen, PA, 1998)

Zaloga, Steven J., & Grandsen, Chris, *Soviet Tanks and Combat Vehicles of World War II* (Arms & Armour Press, 1984)

Ziemke, Earl F., *The Red Army 1918–1941: From Vanguard to World Revolution* (Routledge, 2004)

PLATE COMMENTARIES

A: 1922–1924

A1: *Zamkomvzvoda*, Rifles, 1922

This deputy platoon commander wears a standard summer field and service uniform as seen at the end of the Civil War. His 1919-pattern *budenovka* cap is in this case made from yellow-khaki corduroy cloth, and bears the first version of the enamelled red star badge (see also **1a**) showing a hammer-&-plough motif. The badge is pinned through a cloth star in the infantry branch colour of raspberry-red (in 1919 the star was 105mm across, reduced to 95mm from 1922). His 1919 *gymnastiorka* pullover field shirt in sand-khaki linen has had the three 1922-regulation infantry-red *razgovory* tabs added, part of one on the standing collar and two on the chest divided by the buttoned placket. The diamond-shaped patch on his left upper sleeve is one of the four branch-of-service badges authorized from April 1920. Sewn directly to his left forearm are his 1919-pattern insignia of rank ('command'): the red star of all ranks, and the two triangles of a *zamkomvzvoda*. His tapered trousers are made from the same linen material as the field shirt, and are tucked into Imperial Army-issue *sapogi* boots. His belt equipment is minimal, with a single 'Type 1' ammunition pouch. He is armed with the standard Russian 7.62mm M1891 Moisin–Nagant rifle, usually carried with the socket bayonet fixed.

A2: Machine-gunner, Rifles, 1923

This private or 'Red Army man', also in summer uniform, is manning a 7.62mm M1910 Maxim gun on its wheeled Sokolov carriage – a weapon ubiquitous in Russian armies from before World War I until and throughout World War II. His *budenovka* is of the distinctive January 1922 summer pattern in light khaki cotton or linen, with the front visor (peak) and rear sun flap made in one piece like a continuous brim. The frontal star in raspberry-red cloth has black edge-piping, as do the plain patches on the fall collar of his M1922 field shirt. On the left forearm he displays the 1922 rank-insignia tab ending in a 'bastion' or 'duck's-foot' shape; since he is a private, it bears only the red star. Instead of *sapogi* marching boots he wears brown ankle boots with woollen puttees.

A3: Troop commander, 3rd Cavalry Regiment, 1924

The cavalry were the elite arm of the Red Army in the 1920s, and often wore some of the smartest available uniforms; this officer has seen service before 1917 in the Imperial Army, and has maintained a soldierly appearance. Before a new system of unit-coloured peaked service caps was introduced from 1924, most cavalry caps had red crowns piped in blue, with a blue band piped in red. On the band is the M1922 star badge with the new hammer-&-sickle device, issued from 1923. On the chest of his light khaki *gymnastiorka* he displays cavalry-blue *razgovory* piped in black. The matching cavalry collar patches do not yet bear the regulation command insignia (the single red square of a *komvzvoda*), but instead the crossed sabres-&-horseshoe symbol of the cavalry branch, behind an Arabic regimental numeral. On the upper left sleeve of his tunic is a blue cavalry branch patch bearing a red star and crossed sabres against a sunburst within a large horseshoe. His 1922-regulation command insignia of a red star above one red square is worn on the left forearm on a cavalry-blue 'bastion'-topped tab, again piped black. His

blue breeches are reinforced with leather patches on the inside leg, and are tucked into high-quality riding boots with strap-on spurs. His M1911 leather belt equipment is worn with the shoulder braces vertical, as favoured by Tsarist officers (Bolshevik commanders often wore them crossed at the front). It supports a holstered 7.62mm M1895 Nagant revolver, and a Cossack *shashka* sabre.

B: 1923–1929

B1: Border guard, OGPU Frontier Troops, 1923

This private of the strong border protection forces is wearing an early version of the OGPU uniform introduced in 1922. His headgear is the 1919 woollen *budenovka,* which has been dyed dark blue for the OGPU. It bears the 1922 red-painted or enamelled metal star badge pinned through a large branch-colour cloth star, here in the bright green of the Frontier Troops. Greatcoats worn by some OGPU showed darker grey turn-down collar and turn-back cuffs. The *razgovory* chest tabs are green with red piping, as are the lozenge-shaped collar patches bearing the regimental numeral '10'. On the left upper sleeve he displays the Frontier Troops' green diamond-shaped patch; below this is his rank tab, bearing in his case simply the red star. His brown leather belt supports a Type 1 double ammunition pouch; shortages during the 1920s meant that many soldiers had only one pouch, to allow more men to be equipped. The rifle is the standard M1891 Moisin-Nagant.

B2: Junior commander, OGPU Internal Troops, 1927

The junior officer status of this OGPU man on security operations is speculative, surmised from his general

1924: this summer parade by Red Army cavalrymen shows off one distinct variation of the usual lightweight *budenovka* cap; here the crown rises to a high, stiffened point, and it has a very deep button-up ear-and-neck flap (contrast with Plate A). According to one standing joke in the Soviet Union of the 1920s, the taller the point of the *budenovka,* the smaller the wearer's brain. (Author's collection)

appearance and armament, since he displays no rank insignia. He has the service cap with dark blue crown, dull red band, and raspberry-red piping worn by all ranks of the OGPU security and internal troops, with the universal M1922 red star badge, and the black chinstrap introduced in 1927. (The large transport/escort branch of the security troops wore caps with dull red crowns and black bands, piped raspberry-red.) The khaki *French* tunic fastens at the collar with hooks-&-eyes; the collar patches are dull red with raspberry-red edge piping, and bear brass Cyrillic letters identifying the district, behind Arabic unit numerals. Dark blue riding breeches and black riding boots complete the uniform. The 7.63mm Mauser C96 semi-automatic pistol was one of a number of foreign types imported in quantity by the Soviet Union during the 1920s; the M1921 so-called 'Bolo' model with a 3.9in barrel was particularly popular. The OGPU man's readiness for combat is emphasized by the number of spare 10-round stripper-clips that he carries in a total of 12 pouches around the whole length of his belt. The C-96 usually came with this hollow dual-purpose wooden holster-stock; the narrow end could be clipped to the rear of the butt frame to make a shoulder-stock for more accurate rapid firing.

B3: Light machine-gunner, Rifles; Manchuria, winter 1928/29

This *krasnoarmeyets* is serving on the troubled Mongolian-Manchurian border during the winter preceding the summer campaign of 1929. Photographs show fleece caps being worn alongside the winter *budenovka* in the Far East. Like the *tulup* sheepskin watchcoat, these may either have been purchased locally, or drawn from pre-1917 Imperial Army regional stores. The same is true of the gloves, and the composite felt and leather boots. This soldier's weapon is unusual. By the mid-1920s it was difficult to source spares for the variety of ageing foreign light machine guns previously supplied to the Imperial and later White armies; accordingly, this 7.62mm Maxim-Tokarev MT-26 was designed and built at the Tula factory. It was an adaptation of the Maxim M1910 HMG, with a buttstock and rifle trigger mechanism, an air-cooled barrel with a slim pierced jacket and a bipod, and was fed with 100-rd belts from a drum magazine. Only 2,500 were produced, of which most were later exported; at 15.5kg (34lbs) it was heavy for a man-portable weapon.

1930: OGPU Frontier Troops pose with a Maxim M1910 heavy machine gun. The bright green crown of their service caps (see G2) shows up in contrast to their khaki uniforms. (Author's collection)

B4: *Komvzvoda*, 23rd Cavalry Regiment, 4th Cavalry Division, 1928

This troop commander is aged in his thirties, so may be a former Tsarist officer taken into service as a 'specialist' during the Civil War. In 1924–28 a system of coloured service caps was introduced to identify the cavalry divisions and the sequences of regiments within them. This raspberry-red crown piped with yellow indicates 4th Cav Div, and the blue band its (fifth) 23rd Regiment. It has not yet acquired the black leather chinstrap. The shades of the khaki *French* varied, this man's tunic being of a browner colour. The cavalry-blue collar patches, with officers' gold piping on three sides, bear the single square red 'jewel' indicating the equivalent rank to second lieutenant. The blue breeches and officers'-quality riding boots with screw-in steel spurs are standard. His leather belt with two shoulder braces supports a holstered M1895 Nagant revolver and an ex-Imperial Army cavalry sabre.

C: COUNTER-INSURGENCY WARFARE, CENTRAL ASIA, 1920s–30s

C1: Light machine-gunner, Rifles; Fergana Valley, 1927

This very slightly-built young Lewis-gunner has the standard summer uniform worn by the Red Army in the late 1920s and early 1930s in the hot climate of Central Asia. His service cap is the M1922, with the universal red star badge. This cap, like the field shirt, came in a variety of shades of light khaki; here the latter has faded to off-white with exposure and frequent washing. His only field equipment is a belt and a canvas haversack with spare magazines for his Lewis LMG. The M1912 Lewis was among several foreign types (including the French M1915 CSRG 'Chauchat' and M1909 Hotchkiss) supplied in large numbers to the White armies during the Civil War, and retained until Soviet models could be produced in the late 1920s.

C2: Tajik auxiliary, 1927

This native auxiliary has been recruited from among Muslim former Basmachi guerrillas during the long Red Army campaigns in Central Asia. The Soviets were quick to recruit any Muslims of various ethnicities who were willing to fight on their side, and formed units such as an Uzbek Cavalry Brigade. This Tajik cavalryman is wearing civilian clothing and boots, with the addition of a red stripe sewn to his turban as a field sign, and a Muslim left sleeve patch (see also **2a**). A pouch-bandolier carries clips for his ex-Imperial Army Winchester M1895, of which some 294,000 were produced in the USA for the Tsar's army in 1915–17, in 7.62mm calibre and with stripper-clip guides for reloading. Hanging from his belt is a Cossack *shashka* sabre, which would have been given to him by his Russian unit commander.

C3: Border guard, OGPU Frontier Troops; Central Asia, 1930

As early as 1919, the Bolsheviks had created ChON ('special purpose') units, to which trusted volunteers under the command of commissars were assigned for the 'struggle against banditry' – i.e. the anti-Bolshevik peasant resistance movement. While the ChON were disbanded in 1924–25, their task remained, and was fulfilled by the troops of the security agency. This border guard on operations against the Basmachi rebels again (see **B1**) wears the *budenovka* is dark blue and bearing the cloth star in the Frontier Troops' green colour, here edged with yellow. Black leather uniform items were also typically seen among security personnel, in this case apparently an unusual field shirt. While this private's green collar patches lack any command symbols; in 1929–31 some security personnel wore these in the form of small shields, before reverting to the RKKA's geometric shapes. On the breast of his jacket he displays an unidentified metal badge, of which several types were issued during the Central Asian campaigns. The fact that he is a trusted member of his unit is suggested by the fact that he has been issued with one of the limited number of imported M1921 Thompson sub-machine guns available.

D: 1932–38

D1: *Krasnoarmeyets*, Rifles, 1932

Although the production of uniforms from the later 1920s was centrally regulated, variations in their shade continued to be seen, and photographs suggest that detailed compliance with any regulations might be long delayed. This 'Red Army man' (private) wears a typical two-pocket field shirt and trousers in light khaki cotton or linen, puttees and ankle boots, but with a winter dark khaki service cap. The M1922 cap badge, and unbadged raspberry-red collar patches piped black, are his only insignia. His belt supports Type 1 ammunition pouches, as worn until 1937, when a new type was introduced in several different models. In light marching order, he carries a blanket-roll over his shoulder, with its ends tied and thrust into his aluminium mess tin; otherwise he carries only his aluminium water bottle slung in its canvas cover.

D2: *Kapitan*, Artillery, 1935–36

This officer is wearing an originally Finnish-made helmet, identifiable by a 'pommel'-shaped ventilator at the apex instead of the comb of the Adrian type; it has a red-painted thin metal star plate attached to the front. Introduced in the Imperial Army in 1917, this helmet should long have disappeared by the mid-1930s, but, for instance, photographs show Soviet cavalry wearing it in Poland as late as September 1939. The *gymnastiorka* has two breast pockets (often box-pleated for officers) and two hidden 'slash'waist pockets. His gold-piped black collar patches bear the single red-enamelled bar of his rank, but no branch badge. Neither does the field shirt yet display the branch-colour collar and cuff piping authorized from December 1935, but on both forearms he wears the new 1935 rank insignia of a single medium-width red chevron. The officers' brown leather service belt with a cut-out star buckle was often worn in the field, against regulations. This battery commander carries an officers' leather map case and a pair of binoculars.

D3: Motorcyclist, Armoured Troops, 1938

This motorcycle courier still wears the old Adrian helmet despite the introduction of the M1936. His long black leather or proofed canvas coat ('devil's-skin') divides and buttons around the legs for protection when riding. Motorized and motorcycle units were dispersed within formations, and bore the colours of the branch to which they were attached. This *yefreytor* serves with an armoured brigade, and wears that branch's black collar patches piped with red, displaying his triangle of rank below the winged wheels symbol of motorized troops. The PPD-34 sub-machine gun, introduced to the RKKA in 1935, was based on the German MP28; it took a 7.62mm pistol round, fed from a 25-rd curved box magazine. Only some 4,000 of the initial model were produced, and issued to elite units such as NKVD security and frontier

1937: this police sergeant-equivalent of the Militia wears a dark blue peaked cap piped in red, reportedly with a lighter blue band; his collar patches are certainly light blue (see G1). On his left breast is an award showing that he is ready for 'Labour & Defence' duties. The leather cross-strap from his left shoulder shows that he is armed with a holstered revolver or pistol. (Author's collection)

troops; they were obviously handy for motorcyclists. Later PPD-34/38 and PPD-40 modifications brought production up to about 90,000 before it was replaced with the superior PPSh-41.

E: 1936–40

E1: Light machine-gunner, Rifles, 1940

Although the dark blue trousers indicate parade uniform, this private takes part in a gas-alert drill – perhaps public demonstration? His steel helmet is still of the Adrian type, of the 1930 model; some had this painted star plate attached, but others were beginning to have a star outline stencilled in red paint. He wears the standard-issue BN gasmask, with its filter canister in the canvas bag slung to his hip. The collar patches of his M1935 *gymnastiorka* are in infantry raspberry-red edged with black piping on three sides, and have recently acquired the crossed-rifles-&-target branch badge finally authorized that summer. His weapon is the 7.62mm DP light machine-gun, which reached the Red Army in 1928 and was the standard section automatic weapon by the mid-1930s. The canvas satchel holds two of its 47-rd 'pan' magazines.

E2: *Otdelyonniy Komandir*, T-27 tankette unit; Moscow, 1936

This corporal-equivalent wears an M1933 padded leather crash helmet, which by 1941 was being replaced with a more compact model. Most armoured crewmen wore blue or black cotton fly-fronted overalls, with a single pocket on the left breast and right thigh; the legs could be worn either over or tucked into the boots. Goggles were issued, as were brown canvas gauntlets, and crewmen typically carried the M1895 Nagant revolver for self-protection. His collar patches, of the type worn on the field shirt, are in the armoured branch's black piped with red; they display the two triangles of his rank, in front of an outdated 1922 armoured branch symbol (see also 2a). The poorly armoured and armed T-27 tankette still made up a significant proportion of the Soviet armoured forces in the mid-1930s.

E3: Company *politruk*, Rifles, 1938

A unit's political officer was termed a *kommissar* from battalion grade upwards, and a *politruk* for sub-unit grades; this junior grade wore the same two square collar-patch 'jewels' as a combat *leytenant*. Collar patches were the same as those worn by line enlisted ranks, and instead of the line officers' chevrons a single 55mm red star was worn on the left forearm. Otherwise political officers wore the same basic uniform as line officers, and this *politruk* even displays (against regulations) line officers' red piping on his *pilotka* cap and his collar and cuffs. With his khaki field shirt he chooses to wear dark blue service breeches. On his left breast he displays two awards: that on his right is the Order of the Red Star, which might be awarded for any notable contribution to national defence, while the other is one awarded to participants in the 1929 Sino-Russian War. His officer's M1935 service belt supports a holstered 7.62mm Tokarev TT-33 semi-automatic pistol.

F: SOVIET FAR EAST, 1938–39

F1: *Leytenant*, Anti-Tank Artillery, 32nd Rifle Division; Lake Khasan, July 1938

In the heat of the Mongolian summer this officer wears a version of the hot-weather field uniform. What became the general-issue M1938 *panama* sun hat was already available in limited numbers in this theatre; it bears the same badge-backing as the summer *budenovka* cap – a large star in black branch colour. In the late 1930s some specialist left- sleeve patches began to appear; this officer's *gymnastiorka* bears collar patches of branch and rank, two red forearm chevrons of rank, and a sleeve patch in artillery colours bearing crossed cannon barrels, which now identified anti-tank units.

F2: *Komkor* G.K. Zhukov; Khalkin–Gol, July 1939

General Zhukov's initial 57th Special Corps on the Mongolian–Manchurian border was greatly reinforced to form 1st Army Group during July–August 1939. The 39-year-old Zhukov was photographed by the Soviet press wearing this uniform in the front line. His service cap has the raspberry-red band and scarlet-red piping of an infantry general, and his cuffs seem also to be piped. The infantry collar patches, piped gold on three sides, bear the three diamond-shaped 'jewels' of his grade, which is also indicated by the three medium-width gold braid chevrons on both forearms. He displays three awards: the Order of Lenin (awarded in 1936), the Order of the Red Banner (1922), and the Red Army 20th Anniversary Jubilee Medal (1938). His dark blue service breeches have red piping down the outseams.

F3: *Otdelyonniy Komandir*, 82nd Rifle Regiment; Khalkin–Gol, summer 1939

This corporal-equivalent section commander belongs to a raw regiment that was rushed to Mongolia from the Ural Mountains to reinforce Zhukov's forces. It found itself under extreme pressure during the fighting in July–August, and its commander was relieved by a member of Zhukov's staff, but to no avail. The corporal is wearing the M1936 steel helmet, here with long grass attached for camouflage. His light khaki cotton *gymnastiorka* has infantry collar patches with the two red triangular 'jewels' of his rank. In basic 'musketry order', his leather belt supports a pair of pre-1914 ammunition pouches for his M1891 Nagant; the 'Y-straps' are to support the M1930 German-style knapsack, not worn here.

G: POLAND & THE BALTIC STATES, 1939–40

G1: Militiaman, Baltic States, 1940

The *Militsya* or national police force served under an NKVD main directorate designated GURKM, and might be deployed on security duties alongside the NKVD security and internal troops and the Red Army. This policeman's distinctive uniform is made of blue 'denim' material, lighter in shade for the field shirt than the trousers. The service cap is blue with red piping, and bears the universal M1922 red star badge (some sources mention a lighter blue shade for the cap band). His collar patches are light blue with red piping, and bear a single mid-blue enamelled triangle. Police rank titles were a sequence of numbered 'categories' from the basic '1st category' upwards, so logically this is a '2nd category militiaman', equivalent to the military rank of *yefreytor*. He has a painted tin Militia shield badge on the left sleeve. Militiamen were normally armed only with handguns, but might be issued with rifles at need; this man has Red Army belt equipment, with pre-World War I ammunition pouches for his M1891/30 Moisin–Nagant carbine.

G2: Border guard, NKVD Frontier Troops; Poland, 1939

The NKVD Frontier Troops were selected for loyalty and determination, and were deployed on sensitive borders; this guard is taking part in the invasion of eastern Poland in September 1939. The Frontier Troops' service cap has a bright green crown and black band with bright red piping, and these colours are repeated on the collar patches of his summer *gymnastiorka*. At the rear of the patches is an infantry crossed-rifles-&-target symbol, which is similar to the KA's subsequent version but minus the fixed bayonets. Above the left breast pocket he wears an enamelled marksmanship badge. Equipment is limited to the standard brown leather belt with two ammunition pouches for his carbine.

G3: *Kapitan*, Armoured Troops; Poland, 1939

This commander of a company of BA-series 6-wheeled armoured cars is wearing the M1933 crash helmet, and an M1929 black leather three-quarter length jacket. This issue garment came in several slightly differing patterns, and was favoured by any armoured crewman who could get hold of one, but it was far from generally available. On the collar points he displays the greatcoat-type lozenge-shaped collar patch in black, piped in officers' gold on the upper edges; it bears the new brass tank symbol (see also 3a) ordered in March 1936 for all armoured troops, above the single red-enamelled bar of his rank. Rather than the regulation light 'steel-grey', some armour officers acquired matching black leather breeches; others (as here) wore them in black wool. His M1935 service belt supports his holstered Tokarev TT-33 semi-automatic pistol, and he carries a slung map case.

H: THE 'WINTER WAR', 1939–40

H1: *Krasnoarmeyets,* 44th Rifle Division, 1940

By 1939 the M1936 steel helmet was in general service; it often had an outline red star stencilled on the front, but in this case it has received a hasty coat of whitewash. The greyish-khaki padded cotton *telogreika* overjacket was only intended for wear in moderately cold weather, and was of little help in the -40° of winter 1939/40 in Finland; this infantry private must find it no substitute for a greatcoat, especially at night. He has not received the matching *vatnie sharovari* padded trousers, nor the compressed felt *valenki* overboots. He is at least armed with the improved PPD-34/38 submachine gun with a 71-rd 'drum' magazine, giving him good firepower for forest encounters at short range.

H2: *Major,* Engineers, 1939

This major is holding up for a propaganda cameraman a Finnish national flag captured from a shell-smashed bunker during the first days of the war in early December. He is relatively well dressed for the conditions, wearing an officers'-quality dark grey winter *budenovka* cap, a fur-lined double-breasted *bekesha* winter coat over his uniform, *valenki* overboots and officers' black gloves. His branch is identified by the engineers' blue-piped black star badge-backing on his cap.

H3: Ski scout, 1940

By the time of Timoshenko's offensive in February 1940 some lessons had been learnt, and in an attempt to counter the highly mobile Finnish ski units some Soviet troops were similarly trained and equipped – note this ski scout's cleated mountain/ski boots. He has rolled up a greyish-brown woollen balaclava as a cap; long, hooded snow-camouflage coats were issued by the KA, but this scout seems to wear a smock and overtrousers taken from a Finnish casualty. Under it he probably wears a padded *telegrieka* and *vatnie sharovari*. His main weapon is a 6.5mm Federov *Avtomat* M1916 semi-automatic rifle, with curved 25-rd magazine and forward pistol grip. Only some 3,200 of these were produced, the majority of them in 1920–25. The Federov was taken out of storage and reissued during the 'Winter War' as a stop-gap before the introduction of the SVT-40 semi-automatic rifle. In his other hand he holds a standard-issue RGD-33 stick grenade.

H4: Volunteer, 'Finnish People's Army', 1940

Thousands of Finnish Communists had fled their country after defeat in the 1918 civil war, settling not far over the borders, and in an attempt to legitimize the Soviet invasion in 1939 the Russians formed a 'liberation army' from this exile community. According to photographic and textual evidence, these volunteers were given ex-Polish Army M1936 khaki greatcoats captured in September 1939, with new insignia added – here, simply the plain raspberry-red lozenge-shaped collar patches of a rifleman. He wears the standard M1940 Red Army *shapka-ushanka* grey cloth winter cap with false fleece lining showing on the turn-up flaps, but lacking the KA's red star badge. Underneath his greatcoat he may perhaps wear a captured old Finnish M1927 brown four-pocket tunic with a fly front and a deep fall collar. His trousers and boots are from Red Army stores, and he has been issued with the usual M1891 Moisin–Nagant rifle and its brown leather belt equipment.

1939/40: Red Army ski troops pose for the camera wearing their snow-camouflage coats (compare with H3) and the old *budenovka,* though this proved inadequate during the 'Winter War'. By winter 1941/42 two-piece snow suits and fleece caps were certainly in use by troops from the Soviet Far East brought west to relieve Moscow. (Author's collection)

INDEX